Rooted in God's Love

Meditations on
Biblical Texts
for People
in Recovery

by

Dale and Juanita Ryan

To James and Peter

CONTENTS

PREFACE

If every day of your life is "sweeter than the day before," you probably don't need this book of meditations. If all the burdens of your heart have already been "rolled away," then these meditations will probably not be of much interest or value to you. If, however, you are finding that life is difficult—if you are no longer able to pretend that everything is "Fine, thank you."—then you might find these meditations to be helpful. If you are struggling to make sense of your faith, if your are experiencing an inability to manage your life well, if everything is not going according to plan, then you are just the kind of person we had in mind when we wrote these meditations. The truth is that we have no idea at all about how to write meditations for people whose lives are "fine." Our lives are not "fine." We don't know much—if anything—about "fine." We do know something about dysfunction. Something about addiction. And about abuse. And trauma. We have experienced these things in life. And that is what this book is about. If you are struggling with any of these difficult and painful experiences, then this book was written for you.

This book is a collection of meditations on selected passages from the Bible. We are acutely aware that many people have had the Bible used against them—or have used it against themselves. If this is true for you, then you may find it difficult to approach biblical texts with eagerness and hopefulness. You may find yourself anticipating shame or rejection. You may have developed significant defenses against texts which you expect to be hurtful. We urge you to try keep an open mind and an open heart as you begin these meditations. We are convinced that the Bible can be a significant resource to you during recovery. We hope you will find, as we have, that the Bible communicates clearly that God's desire is to restore us to wholeness and that God is therefore both with us and for us on the difficult journey of recovery.

There are many ways to use this book. You may want to read the meditations one a day—starting at the beginning and reading through to the end. Used in this way, the book provides four months worth of daily meditations. Or you may want to focus on topics that are of current interest to you—reading in any order you choose. Regardless of the order in which you choose to read these meditations, we recommend that you read only one—or, at most, two—meditations at a time. Most of the value of these meditations will come as you use what you find here as a starting point for your personal interaction with the biblical text. We encourage you to return to the biblical text after reading each of these meditations. Spend some time with it. What additional thoughts or feelings do you experience as you spend time with the text? It is your own thoughts and feelings that will be the key to the value of these meditation. So we encourage you not to rush through this book—there will be no prizes for the first to finish! Spend as much time as you are able letting each of these biblical texts sink in to your heart and mind.

We also encourage you to increase the benefit of these meditations by writing about your experience of each meditation in a personal journal. You may have perspectives on these texts that are quite different from ours and they will lead you to thoughts and feelings that can be clarified by writing. If you are like us, a single reading of one of these meditations can sometimes leave you with a bundle of confusing emotions and thoughts. It is important to take time to clarify your personal experience of these texts. Writing is one of the best ways to do this. Remember the clarity doesn't come before the writing! Don't avoid writing just because you feel confused about what to write. Just write. Try not to be a censor or editor. Just get the words on paper (or screen) and, in the process, you may be surprised about how much clarity develops.

Another activity that might be helpful would be to write a personal prayer in response to each meditation. We have written a prayer for each of the meditations but your prayer—your specific communication to God—is far more important. Maybe all you can pray today is "Help!" That's a good prayer. Pray that prayer. Maybe no words come today. Let your silence be your prayer. And let yourself listen. Maybe God has something to say to you today. The value of these meditations will increase significantly if you can find a way to use them as a focus for prayer.

It is our prayer that meditating on these biblical texts will empower you to sink your roots more deeply in the rich soil of God's love.

Dale and Juanita Ryan

IMAGES OF RECOVERY

Recovery is a process of healing and growth. But it is a process that can be very confusing. Sometimes there are so many changes going on at the same time that we lose sight of where we are. At other times we become so entangled in the long and laborious process of change that we lose sight of where we are headed. We can get so confused that we can't figure out what "recovery" is for us. We can't picture it in our minds. We can picture dysfunction easily enough. We have learned dysfunction backwards and forwards. We know it well. But what is recovery anyway? What do we hope to achieve? Where are we headed?

Fortunately, recovery is not some set of new insights about the human condition. Recovery goes back as far as human history. God has always been in the business of bringing change, growth and healing to people who are struggling with the most difficult of life's experiences.

The Bible is rich in powerful images that have long helped people of faith to understand the process of recovery. This set of meditations examines some of these biblical images of recovery.

We have been encouraged by the variety and depth of these themes from Scripture. May you also be encouraged in your journey as you reflect on these powerful biblical images.

RECOVERY AS BEING ROOTED IN LOVE

*I pray that you, being rooted and established in love may
have power . . .to grasp . . . the love of Christ.*
Ephesians 3:17

We all have root systems. Roots are life-lines. They seek out and drink in water and nutrients. And they provide stability in times of wind and erosion.

Unfortunately, many of us are rooted in the soil of shame. Roots in this rocky soil become bound. They cannot sustain growth. They are not able to provide nourishment or stability.

Recovery for many of us is like being transplanted. It is the process of allowing God to first pull us out of the parched and rocky soil of shame and to then plant us in the soil of love. In the rich soil of love our fragile roots can finally begin to stretch, grow and take hold. It is a soil in which real nourishment and real stability are possible.

But transplantation is not a simple matter. No matter how gently God pulls us up out of the soil of shame, there will be distress. And sinking roots in new soil will feel like an unfamiliar and risky adventure.

As our roots sink deeper and deeper in the soil of God's love, however, we will begin to experience growth that never could have been possible in the soil of rejection and shame. We will become "rooted and established" in love.

My roots are in poor soil, Lord.
They do not nourish.
They provide no stability.
My roots are bound, Lord.
Transplant me.
Give me grace-full soil, Lord.
Sink my roots deeply.
Give me stability.
Nourish me
in your love.
Amen

RECOVERY AS BEING FOUND

Suppose one of you has a hundred sheep and loses one of them. Does he not leave the ninety-nine in the open country and go after the lost sheep until he finds it? And when he finds it, he joyfully puts it on his shoulders and goes home. Then he calls his friends and neighbors together and says, 'Rejoice with me; I have found my lost sheep.'
Luke 15:4-5

It is easy for us to lose our way. We may start off with confidence. We think we know where we are and where we are headed. And, then, somewhere along the way in life we get lost. We find ourselves alone and we don't know where we are. We get confused and disoriented. We don't know how to find our way back, how to get "on track" again. Fortunately, God pays attention. God notices that we are lost. And, because of the great value God sees in us, God sets out to find us. God searches for us. God pursues us until we are found.

When God finds us, most of us expect God to say: "Where have you been? I have been looking all over for you! Can't you follow directions? What's wrong with you? I don't want to have to come back out here again to find you." But there is no hint of scolding, shaming, yelling or blaming in this text. When God finds us, God is full of joy. God picks us up and carries us home. God celebrates.

God pays attention, notices when we are lost, searches for us and celebrates when we are found. Recovery is the gift of being found by God.

I was lost, Lord.
Alone. Disoriented. Confused. Afraid.
You found me.
I expected blame and rejection when you found me.
I expected you to be full of rage.
I expected you to see me as an inconvenience.
But you greeted me with joy.
With celebration!
Thank you for finding me.
Thank you for carrying me home with joy.
Amen

RECOVERY AS BEING NOURISHED

I have stilled and quieted my soul;
like a weaned child with its mother,
like a weaned child is
my soul within me.
Psalm 131:1-2

A weaned child in the psalmist's culture is a child who can walk and talk. It is a child who for many months has been nourished day and night at its mother's breast. Every time the pain of hunger came, the child enjoyed the powerful combination of having its stomach filled with warm milk while being held in a close, intimate embrace. Messages of love and valuing flowed into the child's spirit while the life-sustaining milk flowed into its body.

Love and nourishment are the soil in which security grows. Weaned children still need to eat. But they are not frantic about their next meal. Weaned children have learned that their needs are important, that they will be noticed and that their needs will be met. As a result, they have grown secure.

Recovery is like being loved and nourished until we can be weaned. We don't grow out of having needs. But as we experience love and nourishment, we gradually become less frantic about our next meal. We grow. We heal. Eventually a new kind of security grows in us—not the security of toxic self-reliance, but the security that comes from nurture. We become less frantic, less fragile. Our souls become stilled and quieted.

Nourish me, Lord.
Nourish me with your love.
Calm the frantic feelings within me.
Grow a sense of security within me.
I want to be able to sit quietly.
Like a weaned child.
Nourished.
Secure in your love.
Amen

*Then we will no longer be infants, tossed back and forth
by the waves, and blown here and there by every wind of
teaching and by the cunning and craftiness of men in their
deceitful scheming. Instead, speaking the truth in love, we
will in all things grow up into him who is the Head, that is,
Christ. From him the whole body, joined and held together
by every supporting ligament, grows and builds itself up in
love, as each part does its work.*
Ephesians 4:14-16

Why can't you grow up?! Parents sometimes express their anger and impatience with their children in this way. But, it is not a shameful thing to be a child. To acknowledge our child-like-ness is to acknowledge our limits and our dependency. It is to make room for wonder, trust and joy in our lives. It is to be curious, spontaneous and playful. If that is what it means to be a child, then we need more of it.

But there is also a sense, as in this text, in which to be child-like is to be immature or unstable. It is a good thing to grow-up. Not because it is shameful to be a child, but because growth is part of God's plan for us. Being "tossed back and forth" is an exhausting way to live. We need to find some way to live without being "blown here and there."

Growing up is hard work. The reason for this, as this text suggests, is that growing up is closely connected with learning to speak the truth in love. Honesty is a central dynamic of growth and recovery. Increasing our capacity for honesty is not an easy process. But, as we speak the truth in love, we will experience some dramatic changes in our relationships. We will know what it is to be secure in God's love—clear about the truth of God's love for us. We will find a more intimate relationship with God—we will "grow up into Christ."

Help me to be a child, Lord.
Help me to face my needs and my limits.
Free me to enjoy the trust and wonder and joy of a child.
But, help me to grow up as well.
I'm tired of being tossed back and forth.
I want more stability than being blown here and there.
I want to have stable, healthy relationships
with you, and with others.
So, build within me a capacity for honesty.
Help me to speak the truth in love
so that I can grow up.
Cause me to grow into a strong sheltering tree
planted securely in the truth of your love.
Amen

Not that I have already obtained all this, or have already been made perfect, but I press on to take hold of that for which Christ Jesus took hold of me.
Philippians 3:12

Some days the desire to be "finished" with recovery is almost overwhelming. It is such an attractive thought. To be done. It sounds so good. Done. Finally. Please, Lord, I want to be finished with my recovery today.

But, we have learned something about our capacity for self-deceit. We have learned that we are not entirely in control of the process of recovery. And, we have learned something about the dangers of complacency. It can lead us back into denial—and toward relapse. There is no more dangerous moment for us than the moment we become convinced that we are all better.

Recovery is "pressing on." We have not "already obtained." We have not "already been made perfect." Tomorrow's recovery cannot be done in advance. And yesterday's recovery, although it has changed and enriched us, is not the same thing as today's recovery. Today's recovery can only be done today.

The process of recovery restructures our lives in some very fundamental ways. We had learned silence, and in recovery we learn to speak the truth. We had learned not to feel, and in recovery we learn to feel. We had learned either not to need other people at all or to be excessively dependent on other people, and in recovery we learn to need other people in healthy ways. These are significant changes. But, they are not irreversible changes. We can go back to silence, emotional numbness and unhealthy relationships.

Recovery is necessarily therefore a new way of life. It is a daily pressing on. It is the day-at-a-time practice of the disciplines of recovery that makes it possible for us to continue to heal, grow and change.

Lord, you have brought me so far.
Thank you.
I am grateful for all I have gained.
But, I want to press on.
I want to continue to grow.
I want to continue to learn.
Help me to press on.
Help me to do today's recovery today.
Help me to press on toward you.
Take hold of me with your love.
Amen

RECOVERY AS BEING SET FREE

*Then they cried to the Lord in their trouble, and he saved
them from their distress. He brought them out of darkness
and the deepest gloom and broke away their chains.
Let them give thanks to the Lord for his unfailing love and
his wonderful deeds for men, for he breaks down gates of
bronze and cuts through bars of iron.*
Psalm 107:13-16

Addictions and compulsions are a kind of bondage. Painful memories are also like chains that bind us. We try harder and harder to change. But sometimes the harder we try, the tighter the chains become. Recovery begins when we recognize that our bondage is too great for us. We are not powerful enough to break these chains. Either we will find a power greater than ourselves to help us, or we will stay in bondage.

Many people find the idea of powerlessness to be very troubling. We want to be competent and self-reliant. And, many of us have had people attempt to "rescue" us in ways that have increased our shame and self-contempt. So, why should we welcome the God-who-rescues? Won't God also shame us?

First, notice in this text that God's intervention is in response to a request. We do not serve a codependent God. God is not entangled in our compulsions. God will not rescue in ways that are shame-full. God knows that we need to be ready to be helped and that we need to cry out for help.

Notice also in this text that it is the God-of-unfailing-love who is our higher power. Because so many of us are convinced that

16

God is vindictive, punitive and abusive, it can be terrifying in our powerlessness to focus on the power of God. We are sure that all of that power will be used against us. But the God-of-unfailing-love is not a vindictive, punitive or abusive God. God is a God-of-tough-love. That's the only kind of love that can be "unfailing." But God is not against us. God is for us.

Recovery is being set free by God's powerful love.

I was powerless, Lord.
I expected you to increase my shame and self-contempt.
But you are a God of unfailing love.
I expected you to use your power against me.
But when I called, you came.
You crashed the gates.
You cut the bars.
You broke the chains.
You are leading me out of this darkness
and deepest gloom
into the light of day.
Thank you.
Amen

RECOVERY AS SEEING THE LIGHT

The people walking in darkness have seen a great light;
on those living in the land of the shadow of death
a light has dawned.
Isaiah 9:2

We know what it is like to walk in darkness. We know what it is like to live in the shadow of death. But we also are beginning to experience what it is like to see. The darkness of denial is giving way to the light of honesty in our lives.

Of course, when you have lived in darkness as long as we have, the light can be painfully bright. We see the truth about ourselves and our self destructive behavior. We see the truth about our refusal of love. We see the truth of our brokenness. We see old pain. We see current behaviors that damage ourselves and others. The light dawns. It is not a pretty sight.

But God does not send light into our darkness to shame us. The exposure may trigger our deep shame, but this is not God's purpose. God's light is like the light of dawn. It is a light that signals that something new is happening. A new beginning is possible. The light that God brings into our dark world is a light of hope.

Recovery is God's light coming into our darkness. The light exposes. We begin to see clearly the ways we have sinned and the ways other people have sinned against us. And the light provides hope. In the light we see the possibility for new beginnings.

Lord, your light hurts my eyes.
It is too bright.
I see too clearly now.
It is too painful for me.
Help me to believe that your light is
not to bring shame
but to bring hope
into my dark world.
Light of Heaven, embrace me with your warmth.
Heal me with your bright rays.
Give me life.
And hope.
Amen

INVITATIONS

God is an invitation-giving God. God invites us and waits for our response.

To be invited is to belong—our names are on the invitation list. To be invited is to be of value—if we don't respond to the invitation we will be missed. To be invited is to be wanted—if we respond to the invitation we will be welcomed. To be invited is to be free—our choice is respected.

Most of us have experienced what life is like with people who do not give invitations. Those of us who have been abused know that not everyone invites or waits for a response. Some people insist, demand, manipulate, force. Those of us who have experienced neglect also know what it is like not to be invited. We know what it feels like to be an uninvited, unwanted guest in life. Experiences of abuse or neglect can make it difficult to trust God as an invitation-giving God.

The Bible consistently presents God as a God who invites—a God who values us and respects our capacity for making choices. God invites us to experience life in it's fullness. God invites us to receive good things. God invites us to place our confidence in divine mercy and grace.

As you reflect on the following biblical texts, we hope that you will experience God inviting you. May God give you the capacity today to hear and respond to these loving invitations.

A RESPECTFUL INVITATION

Here I am! I stand at the door and knock. If anyone hears
my voice and opens the door, I will come in and eat with
him and he with me.
Rev. 3:20

Some people enter without knocking. It happens. Our boundaries have not always been respected. As a result, we have built some significant defenses. Our doors have multiple locks. When needed, they can be latched, barred, bolted, double bolted and sealed securely.

As we begin the healing process, however, we begin to experiment with allowing our defenses to come down. We unlatch one lock at a time.

Nothing is more helpful in this process than having people who respect our boundaries—people who will knock and wait patiently for an answer. So, this picture of Jesus is full of good news for us. Jesus stands at the door and knocks. It is pure invitation. God does not invade. God does not demand. God does not manipulate. God gently, persistently knocks. God says "Here I am. I would like to spend time with you."

Recovery is a process of learning to trust God. Trust grows slowly. We can't do that all at once. But perhaps today we can listen carefully for a knock. Tomorrow we may be able to manage a "who is there?". And, with persistence, we will some day sit at the table with God and enjoy God's loving presence.

Lord, thank you for knocking.
Thank you for respecting my boundaries.
And, thank you for knocking persistently.
It takes me a while to respond
because my doors
have so many latches.
Give me courage this day
to open the doors
of my heart,
my mind,
and my life
to you.
Amen

*Come, all you who are thirsty, come to the waters; and you
who have no money come, buy and eat! Come, buy wine and
milk without money and without cost. Why spend money on
what is not bread, and your labor on what does not satisfy?
Listen, listen to me, and eat what is good, and your soul will
delight in the richest of fare.*
Isaiah 55:1

Most of us have spent a lot of money and a lot of effort on
things that do not satisfy. When our efforts do not result
in serenity, we become more and more confused and more and
more frantic. Into the middle of this chaos and desperation comes
an invitation. God invites us to receive "food" which is designed
to delight our souls.

God's invitation is to people who are thirsty or hungry. It is to
people who are working hard but finding little satisfaction. The
invitation extends to those who have no money or assets of any
kind. God is not sparing or stingy. God is an extravagant giver of
good things. God wants us to delight in the richest of fare.

The nourishment at God's feast does more than please our
taste-buds. This meal is more than mere esthetic pleasure. The
nourishment from God's table feeds our souls with delight. It is
nourishment that sinks down to the deepest places of our being.
God seeds delight in the foundations of our soul. And from these
seeds come serenity, peace and the courage to continue.

God, I'm thirsty.
I have spent my money and energy
on things that have not satisfied.
God, my soul is hungry.
I need true nourishment from you.

Help me to come to you, Lord.
You know my hesitation.
You know how suspicious I am
of such an extravagant invitation.
Help me to come as an eager child
to receive good things from you.
Feed my soul, Lord,
until it is full of delight.
Amen

AN INVITATION TO FORGIVENESS

*Come now, let us reason together, says the Lord. Though your
sins are like scarlet, they shall be as white as snow; though
they are red as crimson, they shall be like wool.*
Isaiah 1:18

There are three common—and very unhelpful—ways of dealing with our failures and sins. First, there is denial. We tell
ourselves that everybody has problems, so it doesn't really matter.
Nothing of any value comes from this effort to cover-up. A second
unhelpful strategy is to blame others for what has happened. This
can range from different versions of "the devil made me do it"
to "I'm just a product of my environment." Nothing of any value
comes from this effort to cover-up. Thirdly, instead of turning
the emotional energy outwards in blame we can turn it against
ourselves as self-loathing. We see ourselves as monsters and what
we have done as unforgivable. Nothing of value comes from this
effort to atone for our own sins.

God invites us to another path. God invites us to be transformed. In order to change and grow we need to face the reality of
our actions and attitudes. We need to understand that our sins are
like scarlet, like crimson. They are life-draining. Destructive. But
we are forgivable. The destructive, hurtful, life-draining patterns
that are part of our lives can be changed. Changed from bright red
to snow white. We do not have to let denial, blame and shame lock
us into destructive, hurtful patterns. We can be clean and sober.
White as snow. Forgiven.

Lord, free me from denial.
The pretense is choking me to death.
Lord, free me from blame.
It's not working for me anymore.
Lord, free me from self-loathing.
The shame is killing me.
Help me to face the truth
about the destructive, hurtful patterns
in my life.
Help me to accept your offer
of forgiveness and change.
Make me white as snow.
Make me as clean and pure as new wool.
Amen

AN INVITATION TO CONFIDENCE

Let us then approach the throne of grace with confidence, so
that we may receive mercy and find grace
to help us in our time of need.
Hebrews 4:16

Many of us find it very difficult to feel confident in intimate relationships. There are many ways to learn that approaching other people is dangerous. It can come from abuse, or criticism, or disinterest. If early in life the people most important to us were unapproachable, then confidently approaching others as adults may be difficult.

One result of experiences of this kind is that we find it difficult to be confident when we approach God. This is particularly true when we are feeling fragile, weak or needy. The last thing we expect is mercy and grace in our time of need. We expect to be criticized. We expect God to say "why are you so needy?". We expect to be abandoned. We expect God to say "I'm busy now." We expect to be rejected. We expect God to say "If only you had more faith or prayed more or read the Bible more or trusted me more." With expectations like this, it is no surprise that we lack confidence when approaching God.

But God offers us an invitation we long to hear. God invites us to approach. And, God invites us to come with confidence. God will pay attention. God will hear us. God will be interested in our well-being. God will respond with mercy, grace and help.

I don't have much confidence, Lord.
I don't trust other people very much.
I don't trust you very much.
I don't expect mercy and grace
from anybody
especially in times when I am this needy.
I expect criticism, abandonment, and rejection.
Thank you for inviting me to come to you.
Thank you for providing good reasons
to have confidence in you.
You are full of mercy and grace.
Every day is a time of need for me, Lord.
Give me confidence to approach you today.
I need your mercy and grace.
Amen

AN INVITATION TO SERENITY

Do not be anxious about anything, but in everything, by
prayer and petition, with thanksgiving,
present your requests to God.
Philippians 4:6

We can hang on to our attempts to control ourselves and others and stay anxious. Or we can let go and let God.

We are anxious because we think we have to take care of everything and everybody. We are anxious because we believe we cannot be happy unless we can control the people we love. We are anxious because life's problems are more than we can handle, but we try to handle them on our own anyway.

God invites us to give up our anxious way of life. We do not have to take care of everything and everybody. We can, instead, let God take care of us. We can bring our anxious hearts and our long lists of concerns to God.

Responding to this invitation requires a great deal of us. It requires that we acknowledge that we cannot do what we have been trying to do. We are powerless. It requires that we turn to God. It requires that we release our control, our anxiety, our very lives into God's care.

God invites us to serenity. "Give up your anxiety," God says "bring the concerns of your heart to me."

I am anxious, Lord.
And I feel guilty about feeling anxious.
And I feel anxious about feeling guilty.
And I feel anxious about feeling guilty
about feeling anxious.
Help!
I am overwhelmed by all I am trying to do.
I need your invitation to serenity.
I bring you my concerns today, Lord.
I bring them to you.
I admit that I do not have the power
to solve these problems.
I acknowledge that you are Powerful.
I turn my life over to your care.
Amen

AN INVITATION TO REMEMBER

The Lord Jesus on the night he was betrayed, took bread,
and when he had given thanks, he broke it and said, "This is
my body, which is for you;
do this in remembrance of me."
1 Corinthians 11:24

People in the recovery process are people with painful memories. We remember our losses. We remember our sins. We remember the sins which have been committed against us. It is part of the hard work of recovery to face these memories, to grieve them and to come to terms with them. But sometimes the painful memories become so powerful that it seems like nothing will be able to compete with them for our attention. The memory of pain consumes us. In times like this we need a powerful new memory that can challenge the dominance of our painful memories.

Jesus invites us to receive a new and startling memory. "Remember me," Jesus says, "Eat the bread and drink the wine and remember that I gave my life for you. I gave my life because I love you. Take this new memory. Allow it to shape the way you think about yourself and about life and about me.

It is not that the memory of Jesus' sacrificial love erases all of our painful memories. Painful memories still have to be faced and grieved if healing is to come. But God offers us in Jesus a memory powerful enough to compete with the most powerful of painful memories. The death-grip which painful memories have had on our attention can be broken by the powerful memory of God's love.

Help me to remember you, Lord.
Help me to find a place
in my mind and heart
for the memory of your love for me.
I want the memory of your love, Lord,
to be the most powerful of my memories.
I want it to be
The Memory
that shapes me.
Help me to remember your love.
Help me to remember you.
Amen

PROMISES

Many of us have difficulty trusting promises. For some of us this lack of trust is the result of our experiences with promises which envisioned a negative future. Threats are an example of this kind of promise. "You'll be sorry, I can promise you that." This kind of promise builds fear in us rather than hope. For others, trusting promises is difficult because of experiences with people who have been unfaithful to their promises. Repeated experiences with broken promises make it difficult for us to trust any promise-maker.

God is a promise-maker. Scripture is rich with the language of promise. But because of our negative experiences with promises we may find ourselves responding to God's promises with fear and skepticism. Fortunately, God is not like other promise-makers we have known. God's promises are an opportunity for us to learn about a new and trustworthy future. The promises of God can give us the hope and strength to persevere through the recovery process. Even though fear and distrust make it difficult for us to allow God's promises to nurture and sustain us, we can count on God to keep promises. God has promised to bring change and rest. God has promised to love us—and to give us protection, presence and support. And God will do what God has promised to do.

May God give you the grace to be receptive to God's promises. May your capacity for trust be increased as you experience the reality of God's promises fulfilled in your life.

A PROMISE OF CHANGE

I will remove from them their heart of stone
and give them a heart of flesh.
Ezekiel 11:19

God promises us a heart transplant. God promises to change us. Our stone hearts will be removed and in their place will be put a heart of flesh.

A heart of stone is a dead heart. It is closed to honest, intimate relationships. A heart of stone is unmerciful with itself and with others. But we do become attached to our hearts of stone. And we find ourselves fearing God's promised transplant. Our stone hearts have one thing in their favor—they allow us to feel strong and to appear strong to others. A stone heart is a protected heart. It seems invulnerable. You cannot wound a heart of stone.

The vulnerability of a heart of flesh scares us. A flesh heart does not seem as well protected as a heart of stone. It can feel joy, but it can also feel pain. You can wound a heart of flesh.

God's offer of a heart transplant is a promise of life. A heart of flesh is alive. Only a flesh heart can feel joy. Only a flesh heart can celebrate. Only a heart of flesh can give and receive love.

God promises to change us. God will remove our hearts of stone and give us hearts of flesh.

I like the safety of my stone heart, Lord.
But it is hard, cold, dead.
It is a heartless heart, bloodless, lifeless.
Remove it from me.
I want a heart of flesh, Lord.
I want life.
But I am afraid.
Give me the courage to say 'yes'
to your promise of life today.
Remove my heart of stone and
give me a heart of flesh.
Amen

A PROMISE OF GOD'S PRESENCE

The Lord replied, 'My presence will go with you and I will give you rest.' Then Moses said to him, 'If your presence does not go with us, do not send us up from here.'
Exodus 33:14-15

God promised to be with Moses and to provide him with rest. But no doubt other people had made promises to Moses that were like God's promise. People had promised to be with him but had later abandoned him. So, Moses' fears were not completely vanquished when God promised to be present and to provide rest.

We are like Moses. We are facing a difficult journey. If God goes on ahead and waits for us at the destination, we will never make it. We need God to make the journey with us. If God does not make the journey with us, it would better not to go. The dangers are too great. The pain, too overwhelming. We will surely loose our way unless God comes as our guide.

Moses' prayer to God is a good model for us. It is not a sign of doubt or faithlessness to pray for what we need—even if our needs are things which God has already promised to provide. Praying for what we need is good communication. If we are afraid that God will not be faithful, we can share this with God. God will not be shocked. God will not punish. God understands that our capacity for trust has been damaged. Honestly communicating our fears to God, will build our capacity to trust God's promises.

Thank you, Lord,
for the promise of your presence today.
If you will not go with me,
please don't send me.
Because I can't make it on my own.
The journey is a difficult one.
The path leads through deep valleys.
And, I am sure to loose my way
without your presence to comfort and guide.
Help me to rest today in your promises.
Help me to rest in your loving presence.

Amen

A PROMISE OF LOVE

Though the mountains be shaken
and the hills be removed,
yet my unfailing love for you will
not be shaken
nor my covenant of peace be removed"
says the Lord, who has compassion on you.
Isaiah 54:10

Mountains shake. Hills are removed. That's how it feels sometimes during the process of recovery. Our lives seem to be in constant upheaval as we change and stretch and grow. In the midst of these changes, the Lord has compassion on us. God's love and commitment are reaffirmed. We may feel shaken. We may change. Things may look different. But we can count on God's love. It is unfailing love—love that cannot be shaken.

God's promise of unfailing love for us and God's covenant of peace with us can provide the safety we need today. In the storm of change that recovery brings, God's love provides an anchor of safety and security. God's love can provide a peace and serenity that will not be removed.

Lord, I am shaken
down to my foundations.
Sometimes I am afraid
of all the changes.
Will anything remain?
Will there be enough left to build on?
I need a foundation for my life, Lord.

For your love, Lord,
love that cannot be shaken,
I give you thanks.
For your covenant of peace, Lord,
peace that will not be removed,
I give you thanks.
Help me to build on the foundation
of your love and peace.
Amen

A PROMISE OF PROTECTION FROM SHAME

Do not be afraid; you will not suffer shame.
Do not fear disgrace; you will not be humiliated.
Isaiah 54:4

Experiences of shame lead to fear. When shame causes us to be afraid we make extra efforts to protect ourselves against future experiences of shame. We try hard, for example, to look good. We focus on controlling external appearances. We also try hard to anesthetize our feelings because of our fear of shame. We focus on controlling our feelings so that other people won't get to know us. If they did they might discover the shame we are trying to hide. In this way shame traps us in a cycle of fear, emotional numbing and covering up.

But if we hide our shame, it can never be healed. Our shame heals when we reveal our inner being to people who accept us rather than shame us. This is not an easy process for us because we expect to be shamed. We do not expect to be accepted.

What a remarkably grace-full experience it is when God says "you don't need to be afraid, you will not suffer shame." We can open our hearts to God and find acceptance rather than shaming. God sees our fear. God knows that we want to run and hide. But it is God's desire to heal our deep wound of shame. "You don't have to be afraid," God says to us, "you will not suffer shame or disgrace or humiliation with me."

I have experienced so much shame, Lord.
So much disgrace.
So much humiliation.
Sometimes I want to hide myself from life.
And sometimes I want to numb myself to life.
Sometimes I want to disappear completely.

Thank you for your promise.
It calms my fears and helps me to stop hiding.
It helps me to stop covering up.
Thank you that when I open my heart to you
I will not suffer shame.
Thank you for the people in my life who accept me
and do not shame me.
Protect me, Lord, from shame.
Amen

A PROMISE OF RELATIONSHIP

I will not leave you as orphans; I will come to you.
John 14:18

There are many ways to become an orphan. Some children become orphans when their parents die. Others become functional orphans when their parents divorce. Other people become orphans as a result of their parent's emotional unavailability. Anyone who has been neglected, abandoned, or abused by people who were important in their life will appreciate what it is like to be an orphan. It is a painful and lonely experience. Orphans doubt their ability to sustain intimate relationships and find it difficult to trust others. Experiences of abandonment leave us full of loneliness, fear and self-loathing.

Jesus understood the acute pain that orphans experience. In this text he responds to that deep pain with a promise of relationship. "I will not leave you as orphans," Jesus says, "I will not abandon you. You will not be without family because I will come to you."

In Jesus we see most clearly that God is attentive and available to us when we feel abandoned or neglected. God respects our needs and responds to our desires for relationship. God calls us out of the brokenness and dysfunction of our very personal orphanage into the community and fellowship of God's family. We are no longer orphans. We are God's children.

Lord, I know about
being an orphan.
I know about
abandonment.
Thank you for understanding my fear of separation.
Thank you for understanding my need for your presence.
Come.
Be present today with me.
Make your home with me today.
Amen

Even to your old age and gray hairs
I am he, I am he who will sustain you.
I have made you and I will carry you;
I will sustain you and I will rescue you.
Isaiah 46:4

There are times in recovery when we feel totally immobi-lized—times when we cannot 'walk' at all. In times like this, God promises to carry us. When we are weary or burdened or disabled, God will pick us up gently and carry us.

There are also times of exhaustion during recovery—times when we can still move but we don't know where we will get the energy for the next step. When we are on long and difficult journeys that require endurance, God promises to sustain us. God will give us strength and patience and hope so that we can keep going.

And there are times of great danger in recovery—times when the risks seem overwhelming. When we are in danger—trapped and overwhelmed—God promises to rescue us. God will pull us out of danger and bring us to a safe place.

God's promised help is attentive to and informed by our specific needs. God will not 'rescue' us when what we really need is strength to continue. God will not give us strength when what we really need is to be carried for a time.

Notice that God's promised help has no time limits. God is not going to grow weary and regret having made these promises. God will be with us today, and tomorrow, and each one-day-at-a-time day throughout our lives even to our "old age and gray hairs."

Thank you, Lord, for understanding
that I need different things
at different times.
Carry me when I cannot walk.
Sustain me when I need to endure.
Rescue me when I am in danger.
Amen

HONESTY

Most of us have learned pretense. And self-deceit. Denial. Silence. Isolation. What we need to learn now is self-awareness. And truth-telling. Confession. Community.

Most of us find that our pretense and self-deceit are eventually challenged by a personal failure, or by a loving confrontation, or by enormous emotional pain. When this happens, there is an opportunity for our denial to begin to give way to honesty. We can begin to pay attention to our interior world of thoughts, feelings, needs and longings. And paying attention will allow us to begin to see our behavior in new ways.

Eventually we can begin to talk about all these things. Usually we start haltingly, with fear and uncertainty. But each new commitment to honesty with ourselves, with God and with other people encourages us to take another risk. We gradually learn the disciplines and skills of honesty. And eventually we will experience the freedom and joy that honesty can bring.

Honesty is the foundation of everything else we do in recovery. It is the unavoidable first step toward change, growth, accountability, healing, trust and love. Recovery begins as we learn to speak the truth about ourselves so that we can embrace reality and heal. Honesty does not mean brutally telling others how they make us feel. It doesn't mean brutally bashing ourselves either. Honesty is not brutal. The honesty we learn in recovery allows us to be respectful, empathic and compassionate with ourselves and with others.

May God strengthen you as you grow in the freedom of honesty.

HONESTY AND SELF-DECEIT

If we claim to be without sin, we deceive ourselves and the
truth is not in us. But if we confess our sins, he is faithful and
just to forgive us.
1 John 1:8-9

Few people will be so overt as to say "I am without sin." Self-deceit is rarely that obvious. It often comes masked in socially acceptable and socially rewarded forms of behavior. Perfectionism, for example, is a common expression of self deceit. We try very hard to look good. Sometimes we work so hard to look perfect that we nearly convince ourselves that it's true. Then, in the moments when we suddenly remember our human condition, we feel shame and self-contempt. And this often makes us want to work even harder to cover over reality with more layers of self-deceit.

But self-deceit will never lead to change and growth. Only honesty can bring change. Recovery begins as we honestly face our failures, our wrong-doing, and our self-destructive choices.

For people who have tried very, very hard to be very, very good, facing reality can be painful work. The courage to pursue taking an honest inventory of our lives is not possible without some source of compassion and forgiveness that can replace our shame and self contempt. The good news is that God is compassionate and forgiving. God freely, joyfully, completely pardons. Because of this hope, we can look honestly at ourselves. Because we can turn to God and find mercy and pardon, we can make a fearless inventory of our lives.

Dear God, I have tried hard.
I have tried harder.
I have tried my hardest.
But it has only led to self-deceit.
Help me, God, I need you.
I need your compassion
to overpower my self contempt.
I need your forgiveness
to overpower my self condemnation.
Rid me of self-deceit, God.
And build in me a capacity for honesty.
Not so that I can be perfect,
but so that I can genuinely change.
And, so that I can rejoice
in your love for me.
Amen

HONESTY AND SELF-AWARENESS

So then, let us not be like others, who are asleep,
but let us be alert and self-controlled.
1 Thessalonians 5:6

The first step toward honesty is to pay attention. In the words of this text, the choices we face are either to sleep or to be alert and self-controlled.

There are days when we would rather sleep. There are days when the emotional numbness of denial seems less painful then the alertness required by recovery. Couldn't we just "let it ride" for a day? Couldn't we just "sleep" for a while?

Sometimes people encourage us to sleep. "Why are you still paying attention to that? It was a long time ago!" Or "Why are you still 'holding on' to that? Just forgive and get it behind you." Wouldn't it be great to get this over with quickly and not have to pay attention to it anymore?

There is a rest, a serenity, that comes from God. But it comes from "alertness" not from "sleep". God's peace is not like the "sleep" in this text. This sleep is denial, it is avoidance, it is distraction, it is pretending, it is death. Being alert means that we allow ourselves to see and hear, to use our senses and mind and heart. It means that we pay attention to what is happening inside of us and around us. The text urges us to be alert, to pay attention. Pay attention, it urges, even if life is painful, even if it is not what we want it to be.

Lord, help me to pay attention today!
Help me not to put my feelings to sleep.
I want to be aware
of my thoughts and feelings, Lord.
I want to be able
to experience both the pain
and joy of life today.
Help me to pay attention.
Amen

HONESTY AND COMMUNITY

No more lying then. Everyone must tell the truth to his
fellow believers because we are all members together
in the body of Christ.
Ephesians 4:25

Honesty is essential to recovery. Honesty is essential to intimacy. But honesty is not easy.

We were not created to be isolated, independent creatures. We were created to be interdependent. We need each other. In order for us to be helped by others and to be helpful to others, we need to practice honesty. That means we must learn how to talk to each other about our thoughts and our feelings and our needs. We must learn to talk about our struggles and failures, about our dreams and our successes.

Honesty is the soil in which intimate relationships grow. It creates the possibility of being known and loved for who we really are. But it is also full of risks. If we tell the truth about ourselves, people may not listen. They may not want to know. They may not understand. They may judge and reject. They may dislike us. They may give us simple answers to unanswerable questions. They may repeat what we have said to others.

We hesitate to be honest because we have experienced these things in the past. Our feelings may have been minimized. Our thoughts may have been devalued. Our reality may have been denied. But in order to grow healthy relationships—in order to heal and recover—we need to begin to take risks. Learning honesty will be a process for us. It will not come quickly. But as we practice honesty in relationships we will gradually become more secure in telling the truth.

I am tired of lying
when it would be just as easy
to tell the truth.
But I am afraid of honesty, Lord.
It's not as easy as it sounds.
Help me to pursue honesty today.
Help me to be honest with you.
Help me to be honest with myself.
Help me to build a community of faith
where honesty is the norm.
Build in me a capacity for truth.
Amen

If only my anguish could be weighed and all my misery be placed on the scales. It would surely outweigh the sand of the seas - no wonder my words have been impetuous.
Job 6:1-3

When we have lived for a long time by the "don't talk" rule, learning to talk honestly and personally can be a real challenge. Our attempts to move away from self-deceit toward honest self-disclosure may be quite awkward. It's not reasonable to expect ourselves to be gifted at telling the truth when we have practiced deceit for so long. Sometimes our words will seem startling. We will feel our pain, find our voice, and the words and emotions will tumble out raw and uncensored. This text calls these "impetuous" words. Another translation of this text calls them "wild words".

It is not easy to break the silence, to talk about what is real, to tell the truth about what we see and hear, to share what we think and feel, to tell our stories. Breaking the silence is like breaking the sound barrier—sometimes it can be quite loud and it can rattle the walls a little. Or a lot. When our misery feels like it "outweighs the sands of the sea," our emotions are going to be intense and our words will sometimes be wild.

Wild words are part of the journey and should not surprise us. Intense feelings sometimes need strong language in order to find true expression.

Lord, I am not accustomed to talking.
I am not gifted at honesty.
I have practiced "don't talk"
for a long time.
And now I need to practice honesty.
Help me to be patient
and accepting of my wild words
even when the wild words frighten me.
Help me to pursue the truth.
Give me the courage I need.
You, Lord, who created the worlds with a word,
give me the words I need.
Amen

HONESTY AND HEALING

Therefore confess your sins to each other
and pray for each other
so that you may be healed.
James 5:16

Sometimes honest confession can seem astonishing, impossible, and dangerous. Because we have learned silence so well, we experience honesty as full of risk. After all, if we are honest, then other people will know what we think and feel. We will be exposed. The appearance of strength and competence we have worked so hard to cultivate will have to share the stage with our weaknesses, our failings, our fears.

When we practice honesty as a daily discipline, however, something happens to us. The promise of this text begins gradually to grow in our lives. We begin to heal. It is not a dramatic, once-for-all-time, quick-fix kind of healing. Nor is it a private healing, a healing that happens only "inside" our heads or in secret with God.

Honesty leads to healing because people can now express their love for us in practical ways. Honesty leads to healing because we no longer have to pay the high tariffs that pretense demands. We heal because the experience of acceptance counteracts the contempt we so easily heap on ourselves. We heal because we are no longer alone. We heal because we are known and loved.

Honesty is a discipline with a promise. We will be healed.

Lord, give me the humility
and the courage
to practice confession today.
Heal me
as I do the work
of honesty.
Amen

HONESTY AND FELLOWSHIP

Rejoice with those who rejoice;
mourn with those who mourn.
Romans 12:15

We have many reasons—often what seem to be really good reasons—to be strong. But if the bottom line of being strong is to constrict the range of emotions which we allow ourselves to experience, what do we gain? We become people incapable of honestly experiencing the emotional realities of life. In this—and many other ways—we manage to avoid the clear biblical injunction to mourn with those who mourn. Our instincts are often to cheer other people up, to look on the bright side of things, to remind people of things they already know to be true. This text urges us to do the most basic of things. When it is time to mourn, we can mourn.

We can also rejoice when it is time to rejoice. It might seem like it would be easier to rejoice together. But this is not necessarily true. People in recovery have often experienced so many disappointments and betrayals that we find it difficult to experience good things. When something good happens, we expect that bad things will be waiting just around the corner. Instead of rejoicing, our instincts are to protect ourselves from the possibility of the soon-to-follow danger. We do our best to "stay calm" so that we won't be disappointed. But again, this text urges us to do the most basic of things. When it is time to rejoice, rejoice.

The full range of life's emotions are to be experienced in community. As we share the most basic elements of life together, as we party together and hold each other in times of pain, we will become a fellowship distinguished by a capacity for honesty.

I rejoice, Lord.
You do not tell me to calm down.
You do not warn me about getting too excited.
You encourage me to celebrate.
"Party together," you say.
I mourn, Lord.
You do not tell me to cheer up.
You do not tell me to be strong.
You encourage me to experience the pain.
"Weep together," you say.
Thank you.
Thank you for welcoming
the full range of human emotions.
Thank you for joy and sorrow.
Give me the courage to weep with others.
Give me the freedom to rejoice with others.
Amen

Recovery is a spiritual journey. Unfortunately, we are often poorly prepared for the twists and turns this spiritual journey will take. We are rarely prepared for the possibility that we will experience spiritual distress as part of the recovery process.

For many of us, our first reaction to times of spiritual distress is to assume that we are spiritual failures. But spiritual distress is not necessarily an indication of spiritual failure. Spiritual distress is more likely to be a sign that God is growing in us a new capacity for relationship. When we protest God's absence, we are expressing our deep longing for closeness with God. When God seems silent, we learn again how much we need to hear God's voice. When God seems distant, we realize afresh our strong desire to experience God's presence. As a result of spiritual distress, our hearts may become better prepared to hear and receive from God. It is often in the furnace of spiritual distress that purity of heart is formed.

It should not surprise us that during recovery we uncover some major struggles in our relationship with God. We may be angry with God. We may doubt God. We may question God. We may long for God. All of this is emotionally painful— but it is the real stuff of real relationships. If we hide ourselves from these thoughts and feelings when they surface, we may be running away from some of the most important healing that we can experience—the healing of our relationship with God.

May God grant you courage in times of spiritual distress. May your spirit flourish as you heal spiritually.

LEAVING GOD

A despairing man should have the devotion of his friends,
even though he forsakes the fear of the Almighty.
Job 6:14

At some point during the recovery process we re-examine our most fundamental beliefs. A long process of sorting, examining and questioning takes place. And, in that process, our relationship with God is challenged. It is possible that our relationship with God will deepen and strengthen in the process. But it is also possible that we will find ourselves pulling away from God. We may find ourselves angry with God, or afraid of God, or unable to believe in God at all. This can be a frightening experience. It can feel like the very foundations of life are being shaken.

In times like this, we need many things. But at the top of the list is our need for friends who will accept us even if we turn away from God. We need friends who will not minimize our struggle or discount our feelings. We need people who will not be shocked when we are full of rage at God. We need friends who are able to hear the deep pain behind our words and who know that this, too, is part of our healing. We need people who can see beyond the immediate pain to the healing that can come.

Even when we forsake the fear of God, we need friends who understand, who are committed to us for the long haul, and who plead with God on our behalf.

Sometimes I feel agnostic, Lord.
I just don't know anymore.
Sometimes I want nothing to do with you.
Where were you when I needed you the most?
Sometimes I despair, Lord.
Sometimes I can't seem to hope.

I need friends who will not abandon me, Lord.
I need friends who will be patient
and grace-full with my anger and fear.
I need friends who will stay with me
as we wait for you to show yourself once again.
I need friends, Lord, who will give me courage
to hope again in you.
Send help, Lord.
Amen

QUESTIONING OURSELVES

How long must I wrestle with my thoughts
and every day have sorrow in my heart?
Psalm 13:1-2

Sometimes our spiritual distress is centered on questions about God. Where is God? Why doesn't God help? At other times our spiritual distress is centered on questions about ourselves. What is wrong with me? How come I am still struggling this much?

Doubts about ourselves can be profoundly troubling. We wonder if our faith will survive the struggle. We wonder if our faith is strong enough. Often we feel like spiritual failures. The kind of spirituality we have been taught does not envision "good" Christians as people who wrestle with their thoughts and who are sad everyday. We think of "good" Christians as people who trust God and manage to smile in the midst of any circumstances. When we can't manage to do this, we question our faith and criticize ourselves.

But wrestling with our thoughts and experiencing sorrow day after day is often a part of the recovery process. It is not a sign of failure to engage in this hard work. It is a sign of courage. And it is a sign that our faith is alive and struggling. People of real faith struggle in life. People of real faith are people who wrestle with thoughts and who feel sorrow in their heart.

Lord, I get so tired of thought-wrestling.
And I am so weary of heart-sorrow.
How long, Lord?
How long does this wrestling and sorrow go on?
Help me, Lord, not to experience
this struggle as spiritual failure.
Help me to see this hard work
as drawing me closer to you.
Remind me today that you are
with me in all of this.
Remind me today that
you understand.
Amen

QUESTIONING GOD

How long, O Lord, must I call for help but you do not listen? Or cry out to you, "Violence!" but you do not save? Why do you make me look at injustice? Why do you tolerate wrong? Destruction and violence are before me; there is strife, and conflict abounds.
Habakkuk 1:2-3,13

Where were you God? Where were you when I needed you? Didn't you see the violence? The abuse? The injustice? Didn't you care? There are times in recovery when we are full of questions about God. The pain of past trauma can be intensified when we begin to struggle with these hard questions about God.

It is important to acknowledge that these questions about God are not academic questions. No theoretical explanation of the problem of pain will soothe our raging, confused hearts. These are urgent, personal questions about God and about God's involvement in our lives. We want to know that God sees and cares and intervenes in our lives. We need God. We need God's love. We need God's help.

It is an important source of encouragement to know that we are not the first to ask these hard questions. There is clear biblical precedent for asking difficult questions about God. People of faith have always struggled with questions like these. We can take comfort and courage from knowing that the prophets also asked urgent questions similar to our own.

God, I am afraid.
I don't understand.
Violence and abuse happen
and you do not stop it.
You seem absent.
You seem uncaring.
I need to know that you see and care.
I am calling to you for help, God.
Please hear me.
Please respond.
Amen

LONGING FOR GOD

O God, you are my God, earnestly I seek you;
my soul thirsts for you, my body longs for you,
in a dry and weary land where there is no water.
Psalm 63:1

When a young child is separated from her parents, she will protest their absence. She will experience sadness, anxiety, anger and a longing for her parents to return. These intense emotions are not a sign of her failure as a child. Her protest is a clear sign of how important her parents are to her— of how much she misses them, of how much she loves them. At certain developmental stages, it is a sign of emotional health for a child to protest separation. At certain ages a healthy child will protest, will be angry, will be afraid, and will long for the parents to return.

If one or both of our parents was in some way absent from our lives during our formative years, it will be easy for us to imagine that God will leave us as well. We may experience silence and distance. And we may find ourselves longing for God.

Just as it is good for a child to protest the absence of a parent, it is good for us to protest when we subjectively experience God's absence. It is good to give voice to our longing for God. It is good to write or pray or talk about our deep need for God's presence and love. We can call out to God. We can protest God's absence.

O God, do not be silent.
Do not be distant.
I miss you when you seem so far away.
I long for you to be close.
I long to know that you care about me.
I long for you, God.
Nothing can replace you.
No one can be God but you.
Do not be silent.
Do not be distant.
Come. Speak.
I need you.
Amen

NEEDING REASSURANCE FROM GOD

*Can a mother forget the baby at her breast and have no
compassion on the child she has born?
Though she may forget, I will not forget you!
See, I have engraved you on the palms of my hands.
Isaiah 49:15-16*

We may experience abandonment from a spouse who turns away from us to their addiction of choice. We may experience feeling like we have been rejected by friends. We may struggle with memories of parents who were not compassionate with us. Or memories of parents who forgot us in one way or another. Sometimes these experiences are so familiar that we expect them to be part of all our relationships—including our relationship with God.

And so we say to God: "You will abandon and reject and forget me just like all the others!"

God responds to our distress with words of reassurance. We are not always able to take in the reassurance that is offered to us. But there are times when it can feel like a drink of cool water to our parched souls.

God says "I am not like all the rest. I will not forget you. Even if your parents forgot you, or your spouse turned away, or your friends left, I will not forget you. I have engraved you on the palms of my hand."

It may not be easy for us to comprehend, but it is very clear. God says; "I will not forget you."

I need reassurance, Lord.
I want to believe
that you will remember.
But I have been forgotten before.
I know you are not like that.
I know it in my head.
But my heart forgets so easily.
Reassure me, today, Lord
of your unfailing love.
Amen

ACKNOWLEDGING GOD

Let us acknowledge the Lord;
let us press on to acknowledge him.
As surely as the sun rises, he will appear;
he will come to us like the winter rains,
like the spring rains that water the earth.
Hosea 6:3

There are days when we feel God's presence. We sense God's love. We see God's power. But we do not always feel or sense or see. There are times of silence, distance and uncertainty. There are the difficult times of waiting for God to appear. In times like this we may find ourselves both longing for God and fearing that God will come.

The longing comes because in our heart of hearts we know that there is no recovery without God's gracious presence. If God does not appear, we are stuck, bound, hopelessly entangled in dysfunction. If God does appear, it will be like the sun rising—we will be able to see the way. It will be like gentle rains which nurture us so that we can grow and thrive.

The fear comes because often we do not see God as one who comes as sun and rain to give life. We are afraid that when God does appear, it will be to punish us, to demand restitution from us, to shame us. Because we have served vengeful and vindictive gods, we fear that it will be the god-of-impossible-expectations who will finally appear.

We do well to follow the urging of this text to "acknowledge God". We need daily to examine whom we serve. When we acknowledge the god-of-impossible-expectations, then we will surely be afraid. But if we acknowledge the God of the Scriptures whose coming is to nurture and give life, then we will await God's coming like the dawn of a new day.

I acknowledge you, Lord.
You are not the god-of-impossible-expectations.
You are not the god-who-is-eager-to-punish.
I know what it is like when these other gods come.
They bring shame, blame and fear.
I do not acknowledge them, Lord.
I acknowledge you.

Come as the dawn of a new day, Lord.
Bring light into my dark days.
Come as gentle rain, Lord,
Cleanse, renew and nurture.
Come, Lord, as the dawn.
Come as the rains.
Water the parched earth of my soul.
Amen

Tough hardly seems an adequate word. Words fail completely to describe the most difficult moments in the recovery process. Recovery has many valleys. Some days we walk through the "valley of the shadow of death." In the darkness and disorientation of those valleys we may find ourselves filled with despair.

There are times in recovery when it feels as if all we have are tough times. We fear getting lost in the valley and never finding our way out again. We struggle with feelings more intense than any we have experienced before. We struggle with cravings for the substance or behavior to which we are addicted.

Scripture offers us courage and hope in the times of our greatest fear and despair. Scripture tells us that God is with us in our darkest moments. We can walk through the valley of the shadow of death because God walks with us. God protects us. God leads us through the valleys.

May God fill you with the comfort which comes from knowing that you are not alone even in the toughest times.

Do not fear, for I am with you; do not be dismayed for I am your God. I will strengthen you and help you; I will uphold you with my righteous right hand.
Isaiah 41:10

Many of us struggle with fear. It is a very uncomfortable emotion. We would be happy to be rid of it. It causes our hearts to race, our focus of attention to narrow, and terrible possibilities to enter our minds. We wish we could banish fear from our hearts by sheer will power. We wish we could simply stop feeling afraid. Unfortunately fear is not dismissed so easily.

There is something about texts such as this one that leave us very uncomfortable. The words "do not fear" seem like a simple command. God says "do not fear". It looks like a simple imperative. Our job is simply to obey. But, we cannot seem to obey. No matter how hard we try not to be afraid, we cannot seem to make our fears go away.

The key to understanding texts of this kind is to see that when God says "do not fear", it is not a simple command from an authority figure. The words "do not fear" are spoken as words of comfort. And they are followed by a specific promise of God's presence with us.

A loving parent speaks to a child who awakens from a nightmare with words such as, "Don't be afraid. I'm here with you. You are safe." This is not a rejection of the child's fears. It is not an instruction to do the impossible. It is, rather, a promise of protection. If a parent says only "Don't be afraid," then the child learns that the parent doesn't understand and the child feels unprotected. But if the parent says "Don't be afraid, I'm here with you."

the child's needs are validated and the child is comforted by the parent's protection.

God comforts us in the way a loving parent comforts a frightened child. God says to us, "I know that you are afraid; and I want you to know that I am here with you. I will not leave you. I will give you strength. I will give you help. I will hold you by the hand so that you will not fall."

You know, God,
how often I am afraid.
And you know the soil in which these fears have grown.
And you know how I have struggled to be free from fear.
Help me to draw courage today from your presence.
Be with me.
Give me strength.
Help me.
Uphold me with your hand.
Still my fears, God of all Comfort.
Still my fears with your powerful love.
Amen

GOD GUARDS MY HEART

And the peace of God, which transcends all understanding
will guard your hearts and your minds in Christ Jesus.
Philippians 4:20

Sometimes it feels like our hearts are breaking. And sometimes we worry that we will lose our minds. Both our hearts and our minds need protection. When we let go of the defenses that have protected us for so long, and we allow ourselves to be honest and vulnerable, it sometimes feels like we will "come apart." In these moments we can find courage in God's promise of protection. God's peace can guard our breaking hearts and our troubled minds.

Notice that God's guardianship of our heart and mind is "in Christ Jesus." It is in Jesus that we see most clearly that God is for us. God can be trusted to guard us because God cares about us. It is in Jesus that we see most clearly that God understands the dangers to our hearts and minds. God can be trusted to guard us because God knows from personal experience the dangers we face. It is in Jesus that we see most clearly God's power. God can be trusted to guard our hearts and minds because God has the resources to do what needs to be done.

The peace of God is not a blissed-out euphoria that helps us minimize or ignore our problems. God's peace does not participate in denial. This peace is not another Novocaine, another fix to alter our mood. It is the gentle guard that protects us so that we can face reality. It is the security that comes from knowing that God pays attention, that we are not forgotten, that God is with us, that we are loved.

Guard my breaking heart today, Lord.
Guard my troubled mind.
Let your peace do its work in me, Lord.
because I am in danger
and I need your protection.
Quiet me with your peace today.
Guard my heart
and mind.
Amen

GOD WALKS WITH ME IN THE VALLEYS

Even though I walk through the valley of the shadow of
death I will fear no evil, for you are with me.
Psalm 23:4

Sometimes the recovery journey takes us through the valley of the shadow of death. It is a frightening valley.

What a difference it makes in times like this to hear God's promise to be with us. It's not that the fears vanish—they don't always. But we experience them differently when we are not alone. When we are alone our fears can become the focus of our thoughts and feelings—they can consume all of our emotional resources. But when our journey is a shared one, fear does not have the same power over us.

God has made a very specific promise to us when we are going through the most difficult of life's struggles. God has promised to be with us. It is hard to say how God's presence will be made known. Our subjective experience of God's presence may vary widely. Sometimes when we least expect it, we may hear the still, small voice of God saying "I am here." Sometimes God will use a friend, a sponsor, a counselor, or someone in a support group to speak to us in ways that help us to remember that we are not alone. Sometimes God will give us a peace that needs no words.

The important reality is that God is with us. God does not come and go in the way our experience of God's presence comes and goes. God does not forsake us. God walks with us. Even through deep valleys.

God, I am walking through
a difficult valley right now.
Sometimes I think my heart
will give way with fear.
Remind me of your presence.
Sometimes I know you are here.
Sometimes I'm sure you have gone.
Are you really here?
Please walk close beside me.
I need your protection.
I need your love.
Amen

GOD IS WITH ME IN THE DEPTHS

If I go to the heavens, you are there;
If I make my bed in the depths, you are there.
Psalm 139:8

Sometimes life is hell. That's how it feels. It feels like we have taken up residence in hell. Sometimes the darkness overwhelms us. Sometimes we hurt so much that we can't imagine experiencing joy or peace ever again. Sometimes we seem to have "made our bed" in a place that God has deserted—a place from which God has turned away.

But the psalmist says "even if I make my bed in the depths, you are there." There are no genuinely God-forsaken places on our journey. There are no places unfamiliar to God. It is a difficult and painful journey, but our lines of support are not stretched thin. God is not at a distance. God is with us.

If God is with us, we can travel through those dark times in recovery—those times in hell. If God is with us, we can hold on through the difficult emotional and spiritual roller coaster of recovery.

No matter where I am, Lord
you are with me.
If I am up today
you are here.
If I am down
you are here.
If I am very, very down
you are still here.
If I am very, very, very, very, very down
you are here.
Thank you.
Even in the terrible times
when I am in the depths
you are with me.
Your presence is a ray of hope
in the dark times of my recovery.
Amen

In the same way, the Spirit helps us in our weakness.
We do not know what we ought to pray for,
but the Spirit himself prays for us
with groans that words cannot express.
Romans 8:26

When we are alone, when our private terrors have left us without the ability to speak, when even the simplest of prayers ["Help!"] is more that our weary hearts can muster—those are the times we need God's Spirit most of all.

It is life itself to know that God pays attention to us. The Spirit of the Living God is with us and is attentive to our weakness. God does not shame us for our weakness. Our weakness is not a bad thing to God. Our weakness is simply a reality. The Spirit's response to our weakness is to help us. God is on our side. The Spirit knows us and loves us. God knows the pain that crushes us. God helps us in our weakness.

In those moments when we have been silenced by life, the Spirit prays for us. The Spirit prays with groans for which there is no language. When we are not able to pray we can find comfort and hope in the promise that the Spirit is praying for us.

Oh God
I need to be reminded
when I feel so absolutely alone
that you know my pain,
you know my weakness.

When I come to the end of words,
when my mind is full of confusion,
help me to remember that you pray for me.

When I am overwhelmed with despair,
when I want to give up,
when I want to run away in fear,
it is only your presence,
gentle, powerful Friend,
that gives me hope and strength.

I need your help today.
I need you to pray for me.
Amen

GOD PROTECTS ME

When you pass through the waters, I will be with you;
and when you pass through the rivers,
they will not sweep over you.
Isaiah 43:2

There are times in the recovery process when it feels like we will drown in sorrow. The losses, the betrayals, the failures threaten to overwhelm us. The intensity of the emotional pain frightens us in times like this. We feel ourselves loosing ground as life swirls around us.

This text states with great clarity two central truths which are critical to our survival in times like this. First, God has made a very specific promise to us. God says; "I will be with you." This may not always be what we want. We may want God to take the floods of life away. We may want God to build dams upstream in life so that the danger of flood is diminished. But, God's promise is clear. I will be with you.

Secondly, this text says very clearly; "When you pass through the waters, they will not sweep over you." God will protect us and see us through. There are times in recovery when there just doesn't seem to be any way to make it. Nothing is more painful in these times than to have someone who stands at a distance express optimism about our recovery in a way that minimizes the struggle. ["Oh, you're going to be fine. Stop worrying about it."] Conversely, nothing is more valuable in these times than to have someone with us who sees the danger clearly but who is able to protect us and see us through.

For your promise to be with me
in the floods of life, God,
I give you thanks.
Help me to sense your presence.
For your hopefulness
about my recovery,
I give you thanks.
Help me to share in your hope.
You are Life-Preserver to me, God.
Thank you.
Amen

GOD LEADS ME WHEN I CAN'T SEE

I will lead the blind by ways they have not known,
along unfamiliar paths I will guide them,
I will turn the darkness into light before them
and make the rough places smooth.
These are the things I will do;
I will not forsake them.
Isaiah 42:16

God leads blind people along unfamiliar paths. God promises to make rough places smooth for sightless and disoriented people. God will not forsake them.

During recovery we often feel sightless and disoriented. Our abilities to see clearly are often very limited—we don't have enough distance on things to give proper perspective. Denial leaves us blind. Rejected emotions and ignored human needs can also contribute to spiritual and psychological blindness.

So many things in recovery are unfamiliar to us. We are not accustomed to feeling what we feel, to talking about our experiences, or to trusting other people. Honesty is new territory for us. All of this is not only unfamiliar territory, it is scary territory as well.

But it is exactly to people like us that God makes promises. God makes promises to sightless and disoriented people. God will guide. God will give light. God will smooth the rough places. God will not abandon.

I can't see very well, Lord.
I certainly am not familiar
with this path, Lord.
Are you sure you know where this leads?
This feels like a pretty rough trail to me, Lord.
Are you sure we can make it?

Be my guide, Lord, I am afraid.
I would be lost without you.
I cannot find my way alone.
Guide me, Lord.
Turn darkness into light.
Make the rough places smooth.
Do not forsake me.
Amen

When we were children, our parents and other important adults served as mirrors for us. They taught us who we were by the ways they "mirrored" reality for us. We then internalized these perspectives and carried them with us into our adult lives.

If neglect, abuse, criticism or smothering were what we experienced as children, then we are likely to see ourselves in negative ways as adults. Neglect teaches children that they are uninteresting and unimportant. Criticism teaches children that they are never good enough or that they are valuable only if they achieve perfection. Smothering teaches children that they are incompetent and that they are valuable only as an extension of the parent. Abuse teaches children that they are worthless and that something must be terrible wrong with them.

In order to heal from distorted images of ourselves we need a frame of reference outside of ourselves with which to compare our negative self-image. Healing begins when we allow ourselves to see ourselves as God sees us. God can "mirror" reality for us. The good news is that God does not neglect or criticize or smother or abuse. God is a parent who loves, respects and values us. God can provide a new and very different kind of mirror for us. As we gradually internalize the attitudes God has toward us, we will find ourselves seeing ourselves in new ways.

May God's love for you help you to see yourself as lovable. May the value God places on you help you to see yourself as valuable. And may your participation in the work of God's kingdom help you to see yourself as competent.

*"I will set out and go back to my father and say to him:
'Father, I have sinned against heaven and against you. I am
no longer worthy to be called your son'. . . But while he was
still a long way off, his father saw him and was filled with
compassion for him."*
Luke 15:18-20

It is difficult to think and feel about ourselves in Godly ways. Many of us think that the prodigal son got it right. He had a well-practiced speech: "I am no longer worthy." How like our speeches to ourselves! If we hear about our unworthiness often enough, especially in childhood, and if we internalize the speech thoroughly, it becomes a part of us. Many of us know this particular speech so well that we can feel unworthy for no particular reason. We do not feel unworthy because of something we have done or said. We feel unworthy because of who we are. Many of us even think that the more unworthy we feel, the more likely the Father will be to welcome us back home!

But the Father responds quite differently from the prodigal's expectations. The Father was "filled with compassion" and he ran to his son and he kissed him. When the prodigal finally got his speech out, the Father did not spend time arguing the point. Instead he honored the son with a robe, a ring and a party. He treated the prodigal in ways designed to build a very different kind of self understanding.

Our goal is to learn to think and feel about ourselves in ways that are consistent with the way God thinks and feels about us. God's perspective is a surprising contrast to our own. God does not join our internal chorus which is so persistent at proclaiming our unworthiness. Instead God says "You are my child. You are loved!"

Lord, I have not learned
to think and feel about myself
in healthy ways.
Teach me to think and feel about myself
in ways that are consistent
with the way you think and feel about me.
Help me to listen when you say
"I love you."
Help me to take it in.
Amen

Many are saying of me, "God will not deliver him."
But you are a shield around me,
O Lord; you bestow glory on me
and lift up my head.
Psalm 3:2-3

We receive messages about ourselves from the important people in our lives. We internalize these messages and carry them with us—repeating them to ourselves as if they were gospel truth. When the messages are shaming messages then the internal chorus chants "You are not lovable. You are beyond repair. Even God cannot help you."

This chorus is a chorus of lies. The psalmist rejects these lies. And we need to begin to reject these lies as well.

The Lord is a "shield around me," the psalmist says. A shield protects. It comes between the blows of an enemy and a person's vulnerable places. Most shields are small and can only protect a limited area from attack. But the shield which the Lord provides completely surrounds us. We can let this shield protect us from these attacking messages.

The psalmist also says that the Lord "bestows glory on me and lifts up my head." Heavy burdens of shame, neglect and abuse have bowed our heads. The Lord listens, pays attention and cares about us. God's love counters the voices of our internal shame-chorus so that we can lift our heads. God replaces our shame with glory. It is a picture of a ragged, neglected child whose head is bowed and shoulders are bent. A king sees the child and goes to him. The king gently lifts the child's chin until his eyes meet his own smiling eyes. He asks the child to come home and live as royalty with him. The child is loved, honored, protected. You are that child. God lifts your head and bestows glory on you.

God help me to stop listening
to lies about you.
Help me to stop listening
to lies about me.
Be a shield around me.
Bestow glory on me.
Lift up my head.
Amen

SEEING OURSELVES AS WONDERFULLY MADE

I praise you because I am fearfully and wonderfully made;
your works are wonderful, I know that full well.
Psalm 139:14

We are God's creation. God made us. And what God makes is wonderful.

This may sound pretty obvious, but we probably need to remind ourselves that it is not everything-and-everybody-except-me that is wonderfully made. It is everything-and-everybody-including-me that is fearfully and wonderfully made by God.

When we have learned to see ourselves as people without value—when we have internalized contempt as the basis for our personal identity—it is difficult to see ourselves as one of God's wonderful works.

But you are one of God's wonderful works. You are precious to God. You are a unique, irreplaceable expression of God's creative love.

It is good to praise God for making us. It is good to see ourselves as a reason for thanksgiving and awe. God made our minds, our emotions, our needs, our bodies, our creativity, our longings, our hopes. God is a marvelous creator who made us wonderfully.

You are one of God's wonderful works. You can praise God that he made you wonderfully.

Thank you,
Creator God,
that you made me
and that all that you make
is wonderful
including me.
Amen

Look at the birds of the air;
they do not sow or reap or store away in barns,
and yet your heavenly Father feeds them.
Are you not much more valuable then they?
Matthew 6:26

Many of us learn early in life that we need to earn our sense of value. For some, value was earned by entertaining people with our clowning acts. For others, value came from taking care of everyone else. And for others, value was derived from achieving success of some kind. But often there is no way to entertain enough, take care enough or achieve enough to meet our needs for approval. No matter how compulsively we entertain, or care or work, we still are not able to feel valued. These substitutes do not meet the deepest longings of our heart. In addition we run the risk of becoming compulsively attached to these substitutes because we fear that the sense of value which they offer is our only hope of finding peace.

The longing to experience ourselves as valued is a fundamental human need. The need is really a need to be heard, seen, enjoyed and loved by others for who we are rather than for what we do. No amount of earned approval can meet this need. We long to know that we have value simply because we exist. This kind of value cannot be earned, it must be received as a gift.

Jesus says to us "You are valuable. Simply because you are, you are valuable." The birds of the air are God's creatures. God sees them and cares for them. God made them and God enjoys them. They are valuable. You, too, are God's creation, made and known by God. God sees you and cares for you. You are of great value.

As we grow in our awareness that our true value is a gift already given to us by God, we can begin to let go of the tight hold we have on our substitute strategies for achieving worth.

Father, you know how attached
I have become to earning my sense of value.
But, I can never seem to work hard enough.
Thank you, Creator God,
for valuing
the birds of the air.
Thank you, Creator God,
for valuing
me.
Help me to receive this good gift from you.
Help me to see myself as valuable in your eyes.
Amen

SEEING OURSELVES AS BELONGING

*Fear not, for I have redeemed you; I have summoned you by
name; you are mine.*
Isaiah 43:1

Abandoned. Neglected. Alone. Many of us share these painful struggles. Unfortunately, many of us have struggled with them from very early in life. People from dysfunctional families often feel that they were never acceptable to their parents. Many struggle with the feeling that they can never be good enough to receive attention. If reinforced by rejection or abandonment from friends, colleagues, or other significant people in our lives, we can easily conclude that we don't really belong at all.

Humans have a deep longing to belong—to be emotionally bonded with others. Social isolation can be very painful. But social isolation may have felt like the only option available to us as children. Attempts at closeness may have meant experiencing control, abuse, rejection or loss. We may have pulled away to protect ourselves, even though it left us lonely and afraid.

God comes to our lonely, anxious hearts and whispers our name. God says "I see both the fear you have of closeness and the deep longing you have to belong. I have come to comfort you and to respond to your need. I have been seeking relationship with you. You belong. You belong to me. You are my child."

It may frighten us—this invitation to belong to God—even though we long for it. It may frighten us because we expect pain, disappointment, over-control and rejection. But gradually, as we continue the healing process, we can allow God to meet this deep need. We can allow ourselves to belong more and more to God.

Help me, God, to allow myself
to belong to you.
Thank you for calling me
by name.
Thank you for saying
'you are mine'.
I want to belong to you, God.
Help me to heal, Great Physician,
so that I can accept
my place in your family.
Take away my fear, Father.
Give me the courage
to belong to you.
Amen

SEEING OURSELVES AS CAPABLE

*For we are God's workmanship,
created in Christ Jesus to do good works,
which God prepared in advance
for us to do.
Ephesians 2:10*

God is a very capable craftsman. God's workmanship is of the highest quality. We are God's workmanship. We are the art of a competent Creator.

Notice in this text that our creation "in Christ Jesus" means that we are competent as well. We are like our Creator in that we have been created "to do good works." God who is capable of good works made us to be capable of doing good works as well.

This is quite a contrast to "you can't do anything right." In dysfunctional families and institutions people learn to doubt their competence. This doubt leads many people to work harder and harder to demonstrate their abilities. In dysfunctional systems, however, no matter how hard we try, we can't try hard enough. We learn that our problem is not that we are human and occasionally make mistakes but that we are incompetent people. We learn that we are flawed in a most basic way. No matter how compulsively we try, we can't ever get it right.

This text is an affirmation of our competence—of our importance in God's plans. God affirms us by saying "there are good things for you to do, and I believe you can do them." Notice that the text does not say that we need to do good works to earn God's love or to win God's approval or that we have to do the work perfectly or compulsively. What is does say is that God sees each of us as capable of good works. God invites us to participate in the creative, redemptive work that God is doing in the world. God sees us as capable.

You are competent, God.
Your works are good works.
It amazes me that you see me as competent.
Thank you for believing in me.
Help me to trust your words of affirmation.
Help me to find joy in doing good.
Amen

*This then is how we know that we belong to the truth, and
how we set our hearts at rest in his presence whenever our
hearts condemn us. For God is greater than our hearts, and
he knows everything.*
I John 3:19-20

Sometimes it is difficult to believe that we "belong to the truth". Sometimes it is difficult to imagine having our "hearts at rest." The part of our heart that is damaged by shame reminds us of all our inadequacies and failures. As this text puts it; "our hearts condemn us."

In the process of recovery many of us become aware that we have internalized a voice of shame and self-condemnation. We may tell ourselves that we are unlovable. Or, we may tell ourselves that we are worthless. Or, we may tell ourselves that we are not capable. These are some of the ways we condemn ourselves. We also may question our faith. We may wonder, as this verse puts it, whether "we belong to the truth." Because of our early experiences of rejection and our current self-condemnation, we find ourselves expecting God to condemn us. As a result we cannot rest in God's presence.

But God is greater than our self-condemning hearts. God knows everything. God knows our history. God knows the wounds in our past. God knows our humanness. God knows our failures. God knows that we need healing.

God is greater than our self-condemning hearts. God knows everything. And God does not condemn us.

I long to set my heart at rest, Lord.
I long to rest in your presence.
But my heart is full of self-condemnation.
The voices of shame are loud within me.
I am afraid that you will also condemn me, Lord.
I am afraid that you will agree with the shame-voices.
Speak to me today, Lord.
Speak more loudly than the voices of shame.
Be greater than my heart.
Shame can only feed on the hidden things, Lord,
but nothing is hid from you.
Be more powerful than the shame, Lord.
Let me find rest today in your love.
Amen

When our bedtime was eight o'clock we wanted to stay up until nine. When it was moved to nine, we begged to stay up until ten. Not much has changed. We still dislike limits. And when we experience limits as adults, we still make the same kinds of speeches that five-year-olds make about bedtime. "It's not fair. I need to stay up because I have very important things to do. Other people get to stay up later than I do. I'm not really tired anyway. And I promise not to be grouchy tomorrow."

But limits cannot be avoided. We may want to be able to function without rest or relaxation. But when we insist on not being limited, we get sick. We push past our limits at the expense of our physical, emotional and spiritual health.

There is a fundamental spiritual struggle at work here. Our dislike for limits is, at heart, the struggle of a creature who wants to be the Creator. At the heart of recovery for many of us is the struggle to acknowledge our creatureliness. Creatures have limits. Creatures are finite. Creatures get tired. Creatures cannot take care of everything. Accepting the limitations which are appropriate to a creature is for many of us an important step toward accepting God as our Creator.

The disciplines of recovery involve learning practical ways to identify and respond to our limits. It can be enormously helpful in this process to know that God accepts our limits even when we do not. The Creator cares for his creation. God does not shame us for our limits. They are part of God's design.

May God grant you the courage today to face your limits without shame.

As a father has compassion on his children, so the Lord has compassion on those who fear him; for he knows how we are formed, he remembers that we are dust.
Psalm 103:13-14

We are not very understanding or tolerant of our limitations. We forget how we are "formed." Instead of accepting our creatureliness as a good gift from God, we often find ourselves being harshly judgmental and unforgiving of ourselves. This lack of compassion can lead to self-abusive and self-neglectful behaviors.

Fortunately, God does not forget how we are formed. God remembers. God knows we have limitations. God remembers that we are "dust." Because we are so intolerant of our limits, it is important to emphasize that the metaphor "dust" in this text does not imply worthless. It is not that God remembers how worthless we are—just dust to be sweep up and thrown away. Quite to the contrary, God remembers our weakness and limitations and has compassion on us. Again, because we are so intolerant of our limits, it is also probably important to emphasize that "compassion" is not "pity." God does not pity us poor, pathetic, helpless mortals. Quite to the contrary, God's compassion is the tender, loving care of a good parent toward a child.

God knows and respects our limitations. They are not a surprise to God. God is our Creator. God remembers what we tend to forget. God remembers that we are creatures.

Thank you, Lord, for remembering what I forget.
You remember that I am human,
that I need to sleep,
that I need to play,
that I have limited strength and ability.
Thank you for having reasonable expectations of me.
Thank you for understanding my limits.
Help me to be compassionate with my humanness
even as you, Lord,
are compassionate toward me.
Amen

GOD ACCEPTS LIMITED RESOURCES

"We have here only five loaves of bread and two fish," they
answered. "Bring them here to me," he said.
Matthew 14:17-18

Sometimes after reading the newspaper or watching the news
on television we experience an intensely painful awareness of
the enormity of the world's problems and the hopeless inadequacy
of the resources available to solve these problems. During recovery
we often experience these same feelings of helplessness and inadequacy. Our personal problems seem enormous. Our resources
seem incredibly limited. We will need resources more extensive
than our own to make any progress in recovery.

Fortunately, God has a long and consistent history of working
with people who have limited resources. It has been God's consistent pattern throughout the biblical record. God's preference
is to bring strength out of weakness. The abundance which God
brings from a few loaves and fishes is a clear sign of the surprising
resource-full-ness of God. In a reversal of all of our expectations,
Jesus invites us to bring our limited resources to him.

When we see how few loaves and fishes we have, we become
convinced that our needs for nourishment will not be met. And
we conclude that there will be nothing left over to share. But
hopelessly limited resources somehow turn into abundance when
offered to God. There is enough for us and enough to share. Each
day, one day at a time, God accepts our limited resources and surprises us with what can be done.

I am hungry, Lord.
I have not been getting the nourishment I need.
What I have is so limited.
A few loaves.
A few fish.
There will not be enough to go around.
I cannot imagine what use they will be
but I make my limited resources available to you.
Accept my limited resources, Lord.
I bring them to you for your blessing.
Amen

GOD ACCEPTS LIMITED FAITH

I do believe; help me overcome my unbelief!
Mark 9:24

We live somewhere between belief and unbelief. Our faith wavers. At times faith is strong and stable. At times it is weak and shaken.

For many of us, our capacity for trust has been diminished by experiences with people who were not trustworthy. We have learned by painful experience that we will be disappointed if we trust. One of the most intense struggles in recovery is to rebuild our capacity for trust and hope. We want to believe, but we are afraid.

Some people believe that God will respond only to people who "believe enough." "If you have enough faith, God will hear you," they say. But Jesus said; "All you need is faith the size of a mustard seed." The mustard is the smallest of seeds. God does not reject small, limited faith. God will not ignore even the desire to believe. God will not dismiss a willingness to learn to trust. Mountains have been moved by less. God accepts our limited faith.

God does not ask us to wait until we are certain and strong in faith. God accepts us as we are, even with our limited faith.

Lord, you see my struggle to believe,
to trust,
and to hope.
You know my fears,
my hesitations,
my questions.
Help me to accept
the limits of my faith.
Help me to bring
my limited faith to you.
Amen

GOD ACCEPTS LIMITED COURAGE

Trembling and bewildered, the women went out and fled
from the tomb. They said nothing to anyone,
because they were afraid.
Mark 16:8

The most reliable early manuscripts of the Gospel of Mark end with this verse. Mark's version of the Good News ends with this very high drama. Just at the point in the story where we might have expected to find rejoicing, we find fear. The women are afraid. Just at the point where we might have expected confidence, we find uncertainty. The women are bewildered. What a remarkable thing that the people chosen by God to be the first messengers of the Good News were too frightened and bewildered to speak! God chose to entrust the future of the Kingdom to people with limited courage.

God knows our courage is limited. God knows that fear can immobilize us. God does not shame us for being afraid. God has trusted people with this kind of limit in the past. God does not need us to have unshakable faith.

The women in this text did eventually speak. Courage was granted to them. Fears faced without shame will lose their power to immobilize us. God knows that fear is part of our human condition. Our fears do not keep God from entrusting us to be message bearers of Good News.

Thank you, Lord,
for entrusting the Kingdom
to the tired and traumatized.
Thank you for accepting me
and my limited courage.
Help me today to accept my limits, Lord.
Help me to give my fears to you.
Amen

GOD ACCEPTS LIMITS IN MINISTRY

When I went to Troas to preach the gospel of Christ and found that the Lord had opened a door for me, I still had no peace of mind, because I did not find my brother Titus there. So I said good-by to them and went on to Macedonia.
2 Corinthians 2:12-13

Paul was a missionary writing to a congregation that had mixed feelings about his ministry. Under these circumstances we might reasonably expect him to defend himself. We might expect him to say "Things are going great! Open doors! Packed stadiums! Now on several continents! Soon on satellite to the whole planet!" But he doesn't say that. He tells the truth. "There was an open door, but I had no peace of mind." Paul chooses to do honest, straight, appropriate, risky self-disclosure. "I was anxious and lonely and it effected my ability to work. I could not minister to others because I was too needy." Paul rejects the superstar or hero model for ministry. "I can't do this alone," he was saying, "I need Titus."

Like Paul, we have limits in our work and ministry. God does not ask us to be superheros. We may wish for this out of a deep need for approval, but it is not what God asks of us. Like Paul, we will have open doors that we will not be able to respond to because we are too tired, or too anxious, or too lonely. It is part of the reality of being human. God understands these kinds of limits.

Lord, I want to do it all.
I want to be a superhero.
But I am so limited.
Give me the grace to be honest.
Give me the courage to admit my loneliness and anxiety.
Give me the courage to admit my exhaustion.
Give me the grace to be human.
Amen

GOD REMINDS ME WHO IS GOD

Be still, and know that I am God.
Psalm 46:10

We need to be reminded that we are not God. This seems pretty basic. You wouldn't think it would be hard to remember. But we get so caught up in proving ourselves by performing, achieving and rescuing that we forget that we are humans with real limits. We fill our time so full of frenzied activity that there is no stillness. And when there is no stillness, it is hard to remember who is God and who is not.

Fortunately, God does not forget who is God and who is not. God invites us to quiet ourselves—to slow ourselves down. God invites us to be still long enough to regain perspective. "Be still," God says, "and know that I am God."

In the stillness we can see again that there is a difference between our frenzy and God's kingdom. It is God's work to provide and protect and rescue. It is not our work. We can do our part. But our part needs to be respectful of our human limits. Our part needs to actively acknowledge our dependence on God. God is God, and we are not.

Help me to slow down, Lord.
Help me to be quiet.
Help me to be still
long enough to remember
that you are God.
Help me to remember
who is creature
and who is Creator.
Let this truth free me, Lord,
to accept my limits.
Amen

CHANGE

The hardest part of recovery is that it requires us to change. We might be intrigued by the idea of recovery. We might be inspired by stories about recovery. We might be convinced of our need for recovery. These and many other cognitive processes are relatively easy for us. But the doing of recovery will be hard because we must change. And change is difficult.

We understandably resist change. We are angry that we have to change. We feel shame that we need to change. And we are afraid that we will not be able to change. We know that there will be moments when we find ourselves saying "I can't do it. It's too difficult."

But change is also the most exhilarating part of recovery. We don't have to live in bondage to our addictions. We don't have to run in fear from relationships. We don't have to live as if we were responsible for the world. We can learn serenity. We can find freedom. We can experience love.

Change is the most difficult and the most wonderful part of the recovery process. It engages us in a major internal battle. It is not a comfortable battle. But our capacity to change is the key to our hope.

God has given us the ability to change and grow. God calls us to change. God gives us the perspectives and disciplines and encouragements we need. And, as we open ourselves to God's work, God works within us to strengthen us, heal us and make us new.

May God surprise you with your capacity for change.

THE CHANGE PROCESS

We ought always to thank God for you, brothers, and rightly so, because your faith is growing more and more, and the love every one of you has for each other is increasing. Therefore, among God's churches we boast about your perseverance and faith in all the persecutions and trials you are enduring.
2 Thessalonians 1:4

There is no magical formula for change. But there are some helpful principles. First of all, change happens little by little. As this text puts it, our capacity for trust "grows more and more" and our ability to love and to receive love "increases." These changes, like all of the most important changes in life, do not happen as a one-time event. An important change may require us to make a decision at a certain moment, but it also requires a process that takes place over months and years.

Second, change is not a race. The change process can not be rushed. We often want to "hurry it up," but we can't. Change that is real and long-lasting requires patience and perseverance. If we have been practicing our dysfunctions for decades, we can expect that unlearning them will also take time.

Third, change requires that we practice the disciplines of honesty and fellowship. There is no recovery unless we find ways to move out of denial and isolation. What a wonderful gift it is to be able to share our struggles and victories with people who will "always thank God for us" and who will encourage us, affirm us and hold us accountable.

Lord, I want my faith to grow.
I want my capacity for love to increase.
Little by little.
One day at a time.
That's what I need.
Help me to move out of denial
and out of isolation.
Help me to do my part
to make change possible
in my life.
Amen

CHANGING INTERGENERATIONAL PATTERNS

For you know that it was not with perishable things such as silver or gold that you were redeemed from the empty way of life handled down to you from your forefathers, but with the precious blood of Christ, a lamb without blemish or defect.
1 Peter 1:19

Change is not easy. It is a fierce battle. It can be difficult and discouraging.

Change often requires us to challenge the perspectives and rules which have sustained our family system for generations. The "empty way of life" we are attempting to change was handed down from our parents and their parents before them and their parents before them. In a family committed to the "don't talk" rule, for example, saying even a simple sentence may require overcoming distracting behaviors or other avoidance behaviors which have been refined over hundreds of years! Talking honestly to a parent or sibling may be breaking family rules that have lasted for generations.

The Good News is that we have been redeemed from the empty way of life handed down by our forefathers. Jesus redeemed us so that we can be free from this kind of bondage. We can learn to talk honestly. We can learn to experience our emotions. We can learn to trust genuinely. We can engage in life. We can love and be loved.

We live in a battle between the empty way of life passed down to us and the new life that has been provided for us. Living in solidarity with our new life in Christ is a daily struggle, but as we practice this way of life we break the vicious cycle of family dysfunction.

Lord, it isn't just me
that I am trying to change.
I am up against
generations of dysfunction.
An empty way of life
has dominated my family for a long time.
It has been passed down to me.
No wonder it seems so hard to change.
I need your help, Lord.
Help me to find hope
in your understanding of my struggle.
Help me to find hope
in your gift of redemption.
Amen

CHANGE AND LISTENING

He who ignores discipline despises himself, but whoever heeds correction gains understanding.
Proverbs 15:32

None of us enjoy it when people point out that we need to change. We don't like being told that we have switched from one addiction to another. Or, that we are allowing someone's addiction to control our lives. Or that we are running from intimacy. Or that we are behaving in ways that are destructive to ourselves or to others. We don't like hearing these things.

But we need this kind of honesty. We are not wired for honest self-assesment. At the first sight of a problem we experience shame. And our defenses go up. We put our hands over our ears and stop listening.

We need other people to help us see what we cannot see about ourselves. Honest feedback is one of our best hopes for initiating change. As this text puts it, if we "heed correction," we can gain a lot of understanding. So, it is good to pay attention to the "correction" and "discipline" we get from others. We are not helped, of course, by judgmentalism and shame—we have enough of that to last us a lifetime. But we need to cultivate relationships with people who will—with love and kindness—tell us the truth about ourselves. This information can be the starting point for change in our lives.

Lord, help me to build relationships
that sustain honesty.
Give me friends who will love me enough
to tell me the truth.
Help me to pay attention to correction.
Give me the courage
to see myself clearly.
Keep me from shame and self-loathing.
Give me the openness to correction
that makes change possible.
Amen

He called a little child and had him stand among them.
And he said: "I tell you the truth, unless you change and
become like little children, you will never enter the kingdom
of heaven. Therefore, whoever humbles himself like this child
is the greatest in the kingdom of heaven.
Matthew 18:2-4

Children are naturally curious about life. They look at everything, hear everything, want to know about everything. They are ready for growth and responsive to life. But, childhood dies for many people because of neglect, abuse and losses experienced during early vulnerable years. The eagerness and engagement are poisoned. The responsiveness to life yields to fear and shame.

It is possible, however, to reclaim a lost childhood. It is possible to change in ways that allow us to experience the wonder, the awe, the engagement in life that God intended for us in childhood.

God invites us to experience this kind of change. God invites us to become like little children. Children are humble—they have a straightforward honesty about their feelings and needs. This humility makes childlike awe and engagement in life possible. It is a vulnerable, humble thing to be a child. Children get tired and need naps. Children need other people. Children have more questions than answers.

Jesus invites us to change and become like little children. It is an invitation to true humility, freedom and joy.

Lord, I want to reclaim
the wonder and delight of childhood.
I want to be eager to learn again.
I want to be ready
to love and be loved again.
Give me, Lord, the security
and safety I need
to be vulnerable and humble.
Help me to be ready for surprises.
Amen

But hope that is seen is no hope at all. Who hopes for what he already has? But if we hope for what we do not yet have, we wait for it patiently.
Romans 8:24-25

Sometimes it feels like nothing is changing. We feel like we have lost our way—and all hope of finding it again. Ironically we often experience this sense of being stuck during periods that later seem most dynamic in terms of change. Perhaps when change is rapid we are so disoriented that we are unable to see it clearly. In times like this we may not be able to see that anything is changing. It may be hard to believe that all the hard work and effort are worth it. It is during these times we are most tempted to give up.

It is a general truth that we want change to take place faster than it does. We think we could more easily tolerate the pain of recovery—if only we could be assured that it would be quick.

But if we insist that change happen so rapidly that we can see it every day, then our capacity for hope will gradually diminish. If we insist that our recovery always have the drama and immediacy of "miracle," then we will not build the deep-down kind of hope that we will need during the really tough times in life. Hope that you can "see," Paul says, is not really hope at all. Real hope is what sustains us when we do not see change. Hope is the conviction that God has not given up on us. As long as God is committed to us, there is hope for change.

Sometimes I get stuck, Lord.
When that happens, I desperately want a miracle.
I want to change fast, very fast.
But that's not what I really need.
What I really need is you, Lord.
If you haven't given up,
then I'm not really stuck.
There is hope.
Renew my vision of you, Lord.
Help me to see again your hopefulness about me.
And your love for me.
And the joy you take in me.
Let this build again in me a capacity for hope.
Amen

CHANGE AND SURPRISE

See, I am doing a new thing! Now it springs up; do you not perceive it? I am making a way in the desert and streams in the wasteland.
Isaiah 43:19

Recovery involves a lot of hard work. Change and growth take effort. But we are not doing all the work ourselves. God is also at work. God is at our side in the process of healing.

Sometimes, of course, it seems like there is not much for God to work with. We see our diseases and disfunctions clearly and wonder how anything can be made out of this mess. But God is full of surprises. God can turn the most unlikely of events and experiences into opportunities to bring us new life and new hope.

Sometimes recovery seems like a desert wasteland, desolate, unproductive. We can't imagine that anything can grow here. The conditions are too hostile. It is into just such situations that God comes. In a trackless wilderness, God makes a way. In a parched wasteland, God causes a stream of water to spring up. It is a remarkable thing when God finds a path for us when we are completely lost. It is a remarkable thing when God provides nourishment for us in a wasteland. But God does, time and time again.

God is doing a new thing in us. It may be difficult for us to perceive at first. But little by little, day by day, new life and hope spring up. God can take the pathless wasteland of our lives and grow a garden there.

"Do you see it?" God asks "Can you see how it springs up? It will be a garden some day. It will yield a bountiful harvest."

I am not good at seeing it yet, Lord.
Will I bloom and grow?
Will my desert wasteland see a harvest?
Is there a path for me in this wilderness, Lord?
Are there streams of water here?
Surprise me, Lord.
And change me.
Give me the courage, hope and trust
to change a little today.
Amen

GRIEF

The process of recovery is, in part, a grief process. As we recover, we grieve the losses and traumas of the past. And we grieve the destruction which our addictions and compulsions have created in our lives and in the lives of others.

As we move out of denial, we begin to feel intense emotions. We feel sad. We feel mad. We long for things to have been different. We wish it wasn't so much work to heal and change and grow. These intense emotions are all part of the grief work of recovery.

To grieve is to face reality. We face the reality of our losses and, with the support of others, we allow ourselves to feel the pain of that reality. We talk and cry about our losses because doing that allows us to feel and to know what happened to us. It allows us to integrate our losses into our understanding of ourselves, of life and of God. Grief allows us—bit by bit—to move through the pain into new freedom and peace.

As we will see in these meditations, grief is work which is blessed by God. It is work with which Jesus was well acquainted. It is work which the Bible says draws God close to us as God seeks to provide us with comfort, protection and strength.

May God grant you the comfort, protection and strength you need as you grieve today.

Out of the depths I cry to you, O Lord;
O Lord, hear my voice.
Let you ears be attentive to my cry for mercy.
Psalms 130:1-2

Grief is often experienced as being "in the depths." Sometimes it feels like we have been swallowed up by grief. Our bodies ache. Our minds can't focus. Our hearts feel like they will break. Our cry for help during times of grief may seem desperate and feeble. We want to believe that God hears us. We want to believe that God is attentive to our pain. But we feel uncertain.

One of the most difficult experiences during seasons of grief is feeling as if our crys for help fall on deaf ears. Like the psalmist, we find ourselves pleading with God to pay attention. God—who may have seemed so present and attentive when our pain was less intense—can seem strangely absent just when we need God most. When we are in the most pain, we are often least able to experience God's loving presence.

This subjective experience of God's inattentiveness can be terrifying. But it can also be the starting point for growing a deeper and more meaningful faith. A faith that has found the courage to honestly face these experiences of God's absence will be a transformed faith. A faith that has survived a season of grief will have experienced the realities of the spiritual life at a much deeper level. From experiences of this kind we can learn to give up simplistic spiritualities. We can learn to pray with more honesty and integrity.

Can you see me, God?
Can you hear me?
Listen!
Pay attention!
I am calling to you for help.
I am overwhelmed with sorrow.
Have mercy on me.
Hear my cry for help.
Amen

THE GOD WHO STAYS CLOSE

The Lord is close to the brokenhearted
and saves those who are crushed in spirit.
Psalm 34:18

Many people are convinced that when they are broken-hearted—when they grieve deeply over their losses—that God is displeased. God is sometimes seen as a person who expects us to be happy even in the face of trauma and loss. God is someone who asks us to "snap out of it" and "cheer up." As a result, we anticipate rejection rather than compassion.

How surprising it is to hear that the Lord is close to the broken-hearted! God does not expect cheerfulness. God does not reject us. God is compassionate and responsive. God is close—not far away.

In dysfunctional families difficult emotions often result in withdrawal and isolation. It is this kind of emotional distance that we now expect from God. It is not always easy to trust God to be close to us when we are brokenhearted. And it is not always easy to allow ourselves the vulnerability of such closeness. But God is eager to heal us, to restore us and to save us when our spirits are crushed.

When I was angry, Lord,
I was sent to my room.
"Don't come out until you have a smile on your face!"
When I was sad, Lord
I was told to cheer up.
"Just snap out of it!"
Now I expect to be abandoned, Lord.
I expect to be left alone with my pain.
I expect to be lonely in my brokenness.
When I am broken hearted,
when I am crushed in spirit,
help me to rest in your promise to be close.
Help me to rest in your promise to save.
Amen

THE REJECTION OF COMFORT

A voice is heard in Ramah, weeping and great mourning,
Rachel weeping for her children and refusing
to be comforted, because they are no more.
Matthew 2:18

There are times when there is no consolation for grief. There is no comfort. In these times we feel that those who try to comfort us do not understand the vastness of our pain. All we know, all we see, is the terrible loss we have suffered. The world feels as if it should stop. Nothing matters but our loss. We weep and rage and long for the return of what we have lost.

This happened to many of the families living in Bethlehem at the time of Jesus' birth. In hopes of killing the Messiah, Herod ordered that the oldest male child under two years old in that town be put to death. It was into this world of violence and terror that Jesus was born. The Christmas story is not a fairy tale with happy endings, but a story about real life and terrible loss.

There are times in our lives for weeping without comfort, for weeping with anguish and rage. God has come before into times like this. God comes as well into our times of anguish and rage. Because God comes there will eventually be a time to be comforted. And a time to heal. And a time to go on.

But there is a time to weep. It cannot be rushed or bypassed. There is a time for weeping.

God, hold me when I weep,
when I refuse comfort,
when I cannot see beyond this pain.
Give me courage to grieve deeply, Lord.
Help me to tolerate the silence
as I wait for you to speak.
Help me to survive the loneliness
as I await your coming.
Help me to grieve in ways
that draw me closer to you.
Amen

He was despised and rejected by men,
a man of sorrows,
and familiar with suffering.
Isaiah 53:3

Many people have the impression that good Christians are happy, joyful, victorious people. In this fantasy, good Christians are people whose problems seem to vanish when they trust God and pray about it. Unaffected by the pain of life, these relentlessly cheerful people read the Bible, sing praise songs and feel no pain.

Yet Christians are at heart the followers of a man who was named "man of sorrows." Jesus was not relentlessly cheerful. He did not practice a mood altering, pain-numbing religion. He grieved. He wept. He was familiar with suffering. Our God is a God who knows suffering. God grieves.

In those times when we shame ourselves for our sorrow, it can be an enormous encouragement to remember that God is personally familiar with grief. If God grieves, we can expect to do the same.

God, you surprise me again!
When I grieve, I think that
if I could just cheer up,
you would be pleased.
But, you also grieve.
Man of Sorrows
you are acquainted with grief.
Thank you for understanding.
Thank you for grieving.
Help me to experience
your presence
in my time of grief.
Amen

THE GOD WHO GIVES STRENGTH

He gives strength to the weary
and increases the power of the weak.
Isaiah 40:29

Grief is exhausting. Physically we are fatigued. Mentally we are spent. Emotionally we are drained. Spiritually we are crushed. Weariness seems to cast a shadow over all of life. We drag through the days. We are without strength and without power.

Our bodies need to be refreshed with sleep and recreation. Our minds need to be stimulated with hopeful thoughts about our future. Our hearts need to be soothed. Our spirits need to be infused with a desire to engage in life again.

God comes to us in the weariness and weakness of grief with gifts of strength and power. God does not shame us for our weakness. God does not reject us for being too weary to function. We may be tempted to refuse God's gifts either because we want to pull ourselves up by our own bootstraps, or because we don't believe we are entitled to receive good gifts. But, nevertheless, God offers us good gifts in seasons of grief. God offers strength and power. When we can admit our need and are ready to be honored by the Giver of these gifts, they can be ours.

I am weary, Lord.
Sometimes I think I am suppose to stay weary.
I do not feel entitled to be strong.
And sometimes I want to manage without your help.
I don't feel that I deserve help.
Thank you for your offer of strength and power.
Give me strength today.
Give me the power I need to make it through this day.
Give me the grace to accept your gifts.
Strengthen and empower me as I grieve today.

Amen

Blessed are those who mourn,
for they will be comforted.
Matthew 5:4

Jesus pronounced a blessing on people who are courageous enough to grieve. Nothing could be more surprising than this. When we grieve, we often feel like spiritual failures. But God sees things differently. From God's perspective, mourning is valued. It is an occasion for blessing. It comes with the opportunity for comfort.

To be comforted is to be held in the safety of arms you trust. To be comforted is to weep and rage in the company of someone who loves us. The hard edges of the pain are soothed. Strength and hope return in some measure. Healing begins.

Grieving is a commitment to the hard work of facing reality and allowing ourselves to feel the full range of emotions that God has given us. It is painful work. But it is work that is blessed by God.

Father of comfort,
you are my refuge and strength,
my help in times of trouble.
Were it not for your faithfulness,
I would hide from my pain.
I would choose not to see my losses.
I would not be able to face what has happened.
Man of sorrow, teach me to grieve.
Give me the courage to mourn
so that I can be comforted.
Amen

THE GOD WHO IS GREATER THAN MY LOSS

Though the fig tree does not bud and there are no grapes on the vines, though the olive crop fails and the fields produce no food, though there are no sheep in the pen and no cattle in the stalls, yet I will rejoice in the Lord, I will be joyful in God my Savior.
Habakkuk 3:17-18

Sometimes it feels like life is the experience of loss upon loss. There are times when losses are all we can see. We are like this farmer taking inventory. The figs, the grapes, the olive crop, and the wheat are all lost. The sheep and the cattle are gone. There is nothing left, and nothing to hope for. In times like this we are in danger of believing that fear and sorrow are our only companions.

If the inventory of our lives stopped here, then all would be lost. We would be without hope. But there is more to the story of our lives than our inventory of losses can ever show. We can return again to the hope that God is bigger than all of the losses of life. No matter how long our inventory of losses may be, we can find in God a peace and hope that reshapes our struggle. The losses do not magically disappear. But, when we turn our hearts toward God, we know again that there is more to our life story than losses. We do not want the bottom line of our life's story to read "this was a person who experienced many losses." As each day we turn our hearts again to God, we are writing a life story that will end with "though the losses were painful, this was a person who found deep joy in God's love."

Lord, my losses are many.
Help me not to pretend about them.
Help me to grieve, Lord.
But help me as well to turn my heart toward you.
Even as I grieve,
help me to find
joy in you.
Amen

When a leg is broken it takes time to heal. Living with a cast can be very uncomfortable. It takes extra effort. Patience and persistence are demanded from us. But the leg will heal if we allow the healing process to take place. We will walk and run and dance again. In some ways emotional, spiritual or psychological brokenness is more difficult than a broken leg. Admitting that we have a broken leg and need help is not that difficult. It is often, however, very difficult for us to acknowledge that we are experiencing emotional, spiritual or psychological brokenness.

When we are able to face our brokenness, then healing can begin. But we will find the healing process to be much like wearing a cast or going through surgery. We will not like the pain, the hard work or the patience which the healing process requires. Both the courage to admit our need and the strength to endure the healing process are gifts from God. In one sense, healing is not something we do at all. It is a gift we receive. It is God who mends our broken legs and our broken lives. It is God who heals us. This doesn't mean, of course, that we are passive participants in the healing process. It is to us that God gives courage, strength and persistence. We are responsible to put these gifts to use.

God is a healing God. God is aware of our need for healing. God desires wholeness for us. God sees us with compassion. God is gentle and loving toward us.

May God give you the courage, strength and persistence you need today to continue in your healing journey.

It is not the healthy who need a doctor, but the sick.
But go and learn what this means:
'I desire mercy, not sacrifice.'
For I have not come to call the righteous, but sinners.
Matthew 9:12

One of the most remarkable features of the human condition is our capacity to pretend that we are healthy when our lives are in total chaos.

We work hard to cover up our problems and flaws in our character. We will sacrifice almost anything to keep from facing the truth about ourselves. We work this hard to look good because we experience our human needs, limits and failures with deep shame—a shame that drives us to strive harder and harder to look better and better. We sacrifice our serenity, our relationships, our sanity on the altar of perfectionism. We also sacrifice any possibility of getting the help we need by continuing to insist that "we can handle it."

God does not ask such sacrifices from us. God has no need for us to be perfect. Jesus speaks to us gently but very clearly about this issue. He confronts our pretense, shame and perfectionistic strivings. He says in effect "you do not have to sacrifice yourself in this way. You do not have to drive yourself like this. I desire mercy, not sacrifice. I want you to learn to be mercy-full to yourself. Be compassionate with yourself. It will free you to accept your need of healing. It will allow you to acknowledge your longing for me."

Jesus was saying "I did not come to pass out blue ribbons to the people who have all the answers and have worked hard to prove themselves. I came to bring hope and healing to people who know they need help." We can stop shaming and condemning ourselves because God does not shame or condemn us. God knows our brokenness, our pain, our need. We can give up our attempts to prove ourselves and acknowledge our need for help and healing.

Lord, I don't want to be needy.
I want to be strong for you.
But, I can't sustain the pretense any longer.
I have nothing to show for all my efforts to look good.
All I have done is shut you out of my life.
Today I acknowledge my need for you, Lord.
I need your healing and your forgiveness.
I am not healthy.
I need a doctor.
I need you.
Amen

*One who was there had been an invalid for thirty eight
years. When Jesus saw him lying there and learned that he
had been in this condition a long time he asked him,
"Do you want to get well?"*
John 5:5-6

D o you want to get well?! What a shocking question. Isn't the
answer obvious? Why even ask?

One of the most confusing parts of the recovery process is the
fact that we have many layers of resistance to recovery. As we
begin to see the changes which recovery will demand, we begin
to see how attached we have become to our existing way of life.
Sometimes we play games to hold on to the past. We have a good
friend who prayed early in recovery that God would deliver her
from alcoholism so that she could continue to drink! We are all
like this—we want healing but we fear the changes which healing
will bring.

Sometimes the fear of recovery comes from the fact that we
can't imagine any way of being in the world other than what we
have known. A life consumed with despair, rage and self-loathing
may seem pretty awful, but it is the only life we may have known.
Any change may seem risky and uncertain.

God is not ignorant of our resistance to healing. God asks the
difficult question: "Do you want to get well?" It's not always as
obvious as it seems. The Twelve Steps of Alcoholics Anonymous
addresses this issue when it talks about being "entirely ready" for
God to change us. The process of becoming "entirely ready" is at
the heart of the struggle of recovery. Our hearts and minds are
being prepared to answer "yes" to God's offer of wholeness.

My answer to your question, Lord, is yes.
I am ambivalent at times.
I am uncertain and afraid at times.
But, I do want to get well.
The answer is yes.
Amen

A man with leprosy came and knelt before him and said,
"Lord, if you are willing, you can make me clean."
Jesus reached out his hand and touched the man.
"I am willing," he said. "Be clean!"
Immediately he was cured of his leprosy.
Matthew 8:2-3

There is a wonderful simplicity about this story. It summarizes a great deal of life in a few words. A man recognizes his need, comes, kneels, asks, is touched by Jesus and is cured. Many of us are living this story. We recognize our need. We come. We kneel. We ask. We await God's touch. We experience God's healing.

We would like our recovery to be just this simple. We want recognizing our need to be simple. We want our "coming" to be simple. We want our "kneeling" to be simple. We want our "request" to be simple. And we want God's touch and healing to be immediate, tangible, simple.

There are, unfortunately, a few complications. For people who have lived in denial, "recognizing our need", "coming" and "kneeling" are all major changes in the way we normally function. We will need time to grow in honesty, courage, hope and humility in order to "recognize our need," "come to Jesus," kneel and ask to be healed.

What is most helpful in this text is Jesus' clarity about his desires for us. Our Healer wants to give us the gift of wholeness. When we recognize our illness and we come and kneel and ask, then there is no uncertainty in Jesus' response. He says "I am willing for you to be free of this affliction. I want health and joy for you."

I'm not sure you want to heal me, Lord.
Deepen my trust.
Deepen my hope in you.
I need healing, Lord.
But, more than healing, I need you.
Help me today to experience
your desire to heal.
Help me today to experience
your eagerness to heal, Lord.
Prepare me to receive
your gift of healing.
Heal me.
Amen

OUR HEALER HAS COMPASSION

When Jesus landed and saw a large crowd,
he had compassion on them
and healed their sick.
Matthew 14:14

It is foundational to our healing for someone to see us with compassion. We do not see ourselves with compassion. Instead, we often see ourselves through harsh, condemning eyes. We have come to reject and shame ourselves for our need. In order to learn to heal from the inside out we need someone to see us differently than we see ourselves. We need someone to see us as we are and to respond to us with emotional warmth and genuine concern.

Jesus saw. And had compassion. And he healed. All three experiences are necessary to our recovery.

God sees us. He sees that we struggle, that we need help, that we hurt. Our brokenness is not a surprise or a disappointment to God.

God has compassion on us. God feels with us. God is emotionally responsive to us. It matters to God that we are in need. It impacts God.

God heals. Having seen us and having compassion for us, God responds. God touches our wounds. God mends our broken hearts. God strengthens our weary spirits.

For those of us who have felt invisible, who have experienced shame and rejection and abuse, it is a wonderful thing to find someone who sees, has compassion and heals us!

Lord, thank you that you see me.
You see my pain.
Thank you that it matters to you
that I struggle and hurt.
Thank you that it is
in the context of personal attention
and compassion
that you heal me.
I await your healing touch today.
Amen

OUR HEALER IS GENTLE

*He will not shout or cry out, or raise his voice in the streets.
A bruised reed he will not break, and a smoldering wick he
will not snuff out.*
Isaiah 42:2-3

Cheer up! Snap out of it! I thought you would be better by
now! What's your problem?!

When we have been badly bruised, we have an increased sen-
sitivity to noise. Comments like these—which many of us have
heard even from people who genuinely love and care for us—are
a kind of "noise" during recovery. Because we have been bruised,
these comments often feel like "shouts" or "raised voices in the
street." They are a kind of public shaming because of our inadequacies and neediness. And this feels like it will do us in—like the
tiny recovery candle that we have just managed to light is being
snuffed out by the wind of the shout.

And so when God responds with gentleness we are surprised.
No shouting. No yelling. No hurrying to get better. Instead, we
find compassion and tenderness. Our Healer sees that we are like
a bruised reed. God will not break us. God will patiently restore
us. God sees we are like a smoldering wick, ready to go out.
Others might give up on us. But God will work with us until we
burn brightly again.

Gentleness. Patience. Persistence. We need all three. These are
the gifts offered to us by our healing God.

I am bruised, Lord.

I am smoldering.

And, I am so accustomed to shouting.

It's so noisy that I don't always hear your voice.

I don't expect your gentle ways.

I expect you to yell, to be impatient.

I expect you to give up on me.

But you do not yell.

You are not impatient.

You do not give up.

Thank you.

Gentle Healer, teach me to be gentle.

Teach me to be compassionate

with myself and with others.

Amen

OUR HEALER LOVES FREELY

I will heal their waywardness and love them freely.
Hosea 14:4

Waywardness is a turning away from what is in our best interest and following depraved, capricious inclinations. There are many ways in which waywardness can be expressed. Some of us are openly rebellious. We flaunt our wild behavior and laugh at God. Others of us are quietly wayward. We try to appear compliant and good but we are self-reliant and defiantly independent.

No matter how we express our waywardness it is a destructive force in our lives. In our attempts to protect ourselves from any further pain we turn away from God and from others who love us. We shut them out. And we shut out their love. As a result, we close ourselves off from what we want and need most desperately in life—to be known and loved.

God promises to heal our waywardness. God understands that our turning away is the result of some deep wound in us. God sees this. God knows. God promises to heal us by loving us freely. When we close the doors of our heart, God does not stop loving us. Instead God continues to love us generously and completely. God will love us freely until our fears are gone and our defenses can come down. God will love us freely so that one day we will be able to give up our waywardness and allow ourselves the joy of being loved.

Heal my waywardness, Lord.
When I turn away from you,
love me so that I will
return to you again.
Amen

Many of us learn early in life to survive by trying to be self-sufficient. We struggle to be the kind of people who do not need help from others. This kind of toxic individualism has profound consequences for our lives. It causes us to face fears and griefs alone. We try to fight addictions and compulsions by ourselves. We try to be strong. We pretend we are in control.

Unfortunately, this kind of denial of reality is encouraged in our society and honored with misleading names such as "self-reliance." In the Christian community this same kind of toxic individualism is encouraged in many ways. There is no more isolated or individualistic kind of life than one based on the belief that "all I need in life is Jesus." Fortunately, Jesus did not teach toxic individualism. Scripture makes it clear that we were not designed to live isolated, self-sufficient lives. We are, rather, created to be interdependent. We need each other.

One of the basic strengths of the recovery movement is its acknowledgement of our need for interdependence. Recovery from past wounds or from present addictions does not happen in isolation. Recovery takes place in community. It happens in fellowship with others. Fellowship gives opportunity to practice self-awareness, honesty, respectful listening, constructive conflict and making amends. It allows us to come to a place where we can accept our need for others and their need for us. Fellowship offers the joy that can come from knowing and loving each other as people of dignity and worth.

May you find fellowship in your recovery.

FELLOWSHIP AND SELF-AWARENESS

If any one of you is without sin,
let him be the first to throw a stone at her.
John 8:7

It is easy to judge other people. Judgmentalism and blame come naturally to us. Other people's faults and failures are not difficult to identify. Many of us can remember a time in our lives when throwing the first stone was not just easy—it was what we thought good Christians were supposed to do.

One of the most dramatic changes which takes place early in the recovery process is an increase in self-awareness. We begin to see patterns in our own lives that need changing. We see our own self destructive tendencies. We see how we have brought pain to others. As these insights dawn on us, we begin to lay down our stones.

Of course, as our self-awareness increases, many of us attempt to refocus the blame and judgmentalism from others onto ourselves. We can blame and judge ourselves as ruthlessly as we may once have blamed and judged others. But it's not really progress in recovery to give up throwing stones only to then start banging our heads against a stone wall.

Judgmentalism and blame are not helpful in recovery. What makes recovery possible is when increased self-awareness leads to an increased capacity to experience forgiveness. Gradually we learn to accept forgiveness from God and others. We receive mercy. As a result, we begin to treat ourselves and others with mercy.

It is increased self-awareness and the humility which self-awareness makes possible that are the soil in which true community can grow. When we accept ourselves as humans—even though we struggle and sometimes fail—we can become far more gentle with ourselves and with others.

Lord, you know how quick I have been to throw stones.
Thank you for the self awareness
that has allowed me to see more clearly
that I am not without sin.
I know that I am in need of forgiveness.
Give me the courage to accept
your forgiveness and mercy
and in this way begin
to live in true community.
Amen

LISTENING

Listening should be easy. But it is not. At a minimum, listening means that we have to be quiet. We cannot listen when we are talking. Not talking is the hard part. There are many reasons for this. We prefer talking over listening because it gives us a sense of control. We can control the silences between words by choosing when to talk. Since silences of even a few seconds can cause our anxiety to increase, we fill the silence with words even when we really have nothing to say.

It is a remarkable experience to have someone really listen—to have someone's undivided attention and interest. When someone listens, they communicate to us on a very deep level that we are valuable. Their listening breaks our isolation and aloneness. And it decreases the fears which come when our thoughts and feelings are confused. Talking out loud in the presence of a person who listens carefully allows us to gain clarity and perspective. Gradually, being listened to can begin to convince us that we are worth someone's attention and worth being loved.

When someone listens with respect and acceptance we are comforted and consoled. Our pain is soothed. Our burden is lightened.

Thank you, Lord,
for those who listen to me.
And thank you
for the people who
trust me enough
to allow me to listen to them.
Give me the courage
to talk honestly.
Give me the grace
to listen well.
Amen

In your anger, do not sin.
Ephesians 4:26

L iving in relationship with other people means that we will experience seasons of anger. Anger is a normal human emotion. It is an unavoidable ingredient of any fellowship.

Unfortunately, for most of us, anger is a problem. We know that anger can lead to destructive behaviors. Some of us have been on the receiving end of verbal and physical attacks from an angry person. And some of us have lashed out at others with our anger. So we fear anger because we have seen the destruction which results when anger leads to sin. We have seen how anger can damage relationships and lead to loneliness.

But anger does not have to be destructive. We can be angry without harming others. Anger can, in fact, be a constructive force in our lives. Anger alerts us to the fact that something is not right. As a result, anger can protect us and energize us to take constructive action.

The fellowship we need in recovery cannot always be conflict-free fellowship. There will be times of anger. And that can be a good thing.

I am afraid of anger, Lord.
But I know it can't be avoided.
Help me to acknowledge my anger
rather than hide from it.
Help me to use it in ways
that are not destructive.
Let it energize me
to risk and change and grow.
Help me to learn
to live constructively
with my anger.
Amen

MAKING AMENDS

*Therefore, if you are offering your gift at the altar and there
remember that your brother has something against you,
leave your gift there in front of the altar.
First go and be reconciled to your brother;
then come and offer your gift.*
Matthew 5:23-24

The process of recovery increases our awareness of the ways we have hurt other people. For many of us this realization leads almost immediately to shame. And shame leads almost immediately to increasingly desperate attempts to be perfect in order to mask the feeling that we are fundamentally flawed. The downward cycle of failure-shame-trying harder-failure will gradually immobilize us as our self-contempt and depression increase.

In this text Jesus invites us to give up on trying harder. He suggests a completely different and very practical way of dealing with failure. Notice that Jesus assumes that living in community will lead to the need for making amends. The assumption is that we will not be perfect. We can expect to fail from time to time. Failure need not lead to shame or perfectionism because failure is normal. We all experience it.

Jesus suggests that awareness of our failure doesn't have to lead to trying harder. It can lead to honesty and making amends. We are to speak directly about the problem, ask for forgiveness, make amends as appropriate, and be reconciled if possible.

I fail, Lord.
And then I am ashamed of my failure.
And then I work twice as hard not to fail.
And then I fail again. Lord.
And then I become
even more ashamed of my failure.
And then I work
ten times as hard not to fail.
And then I fail again.
Help!
Free me from the cycle
of failure-shame-perfectionism.
Give me the courage
to ask for forgiveness
and to make amends.
Amen

ACCEPTING INTERDEPENDENCE

Plans fail for lack of counsel,
but with many advisers they succeed.
Proverbs 15:22

A friend recently said, "The day my mother told me to lie about Dad's abusive behavior is the day I decided once and for all that no one will ever take care of me but me."

Many of us made decisions like this early in life. For one reason or another we reached the conclusion that it was not safe to need others. One of the longest-lasting effects of abuse and neglect is this kind of ruthless independence.

Unfortunately, because we may not have experienced appropriate care, we have not learned how to do a good job of taking care of ourselves. We are harsh with ourselves. And we have huge blind spots. We keep falling into the same ruts and traps.

The toxic individualism that comes from abuse and neglect is an illusion. We are needy. We need others to help us and support us. We cannot live whole, healthy lives in isolation. We need other people. We need their counsel and their honest feedback. Success is more likely when we work interdependently. We need love and acceptance. We need listening ears. We need to be held accountable. We need encouragement and support from other people. And others need all these things from us as well.

It may seem like a risk to allow ourselves to need anything from anyone. But it is a risk worth taking again and again and again. It is appropriate to be cautious and wise about the risks we take in relationships. But risks cannot be avoided. Mutual relationships of love and care are the basis for all real joy in life. They are worth the struggle and hard work.

Lord, you know the fear I experience
when I allow myself
to receive good things from other people.
You know how hard it is
for me to let myself need people.
And you know I struggle to believe
I have anything to give to others.
So interdependence is difficult.
Help me, Lord, to give and to receive.
Give me the courage to risk love.
Amen

If I give all I possess to the poor and surrender my body to the flames, but have not love, I gain nothing.
I Corinthians 13:3

We need to experience loving relationships in order to heal and grow. In loving relationships we experience the safety that allows us to face the truth. In loving relationships we experience the support we need to begin to change. And in loving relationships we learn that we are lovable and valuable.

Because we have been wounded in relationships, our instinct is often to run from relationships. We don't want to be hurt again. This leaves an enormous void in our souls. And it is this void which we desperately try to fill with addictions and compulsions of various kinds. This text focuses on two manifestations of religious addiction (compulsive altruism and religiously motivated self-abuse) and sums up the result: I gain nothing. The same could be said of all of our addictions. "I deliver my body to be burned" and "I gain nothing" are an accurate description not only of a particular kind of religious addiction but also of chemical addiction, work addiction, sexual addiction and relationship addiction, as well as many other self-abusive compulsions.

We gain nothing for all the time and effort we spend on trying to numb the pain. It does not achieve the desired result. The void remains.

Although loving fellowship may be frightening for us, it is the path to recovery. The vulnerabilities of intimacy may remind us of earlier times of longing for love and being disappointed, but there is no way to recover in isolation. The net result of compulsions and addictions is "I gain nothing." But the net result of recovery is very different. There is something to be gained by all the hard work that recovery requires. Recovery builds in us a capacity to receive love and a capacity to give love to others. And that is a real gain.

May God grant you the courage you need today to pursue loving fellowship.

Lord, you see my guarded heart.
You see the fears that make me run from love.
What I fear is what I want most.
I want to love and to be loved.
Give me courage
to open my heart to love today.
Amen

Have you ever listened to someone express love and appreciation for you only to realize that—although you can hear the words—you are unable to "take them in?" Some people describe this as "having no place to hang" words of love. Others talk about a heart that "can't hold" love—as a broken pitcher can not hold water.

Just the opposite happens when someone expresses criticism. We usually find it easy to "take in" negative messages—they come through loud and clear. In fact, most of us tend to misconstrue even words of honest criticism and appropriate confrontation as messages of harsh criticism and rejection.

Many of us experience Scripture in the same way. God's love is declared consistently throughout the Bible. It is pictured in a variety of powerful images. We can see it clearly in Jesus. But, we can't take it in. Our shattered hearts cannot seem to hold it. On the other hand, if we read texts which call us to replace destructive patterns with life-giving ones, we tend to misconstrue the words as harsh criticism and rejection. We take these messages in and hold onto them. Sometimes we hold on tenaciously. Sometimes we beat ourselves up with Scripture.

One goal of our healing journey is to increase our capacity to take in God's love. As we heal, words of love will more easily find a home within us. As our hearts heal they will hear and hold God's love more effectively. Eventually our hearts can be filled and running over with love.

May God increase your capacity to take in and hold onto love today.

GOD DELIGHTS IN ME

The Lord your God is with you he is mighty to save.
He will take great delight in you,
he will quiet you with his love,
he will rejoice over you with singing.
Zephaniah 3:17

God comforts and takes joy in his children. We are like infants in God's arms. God delights in us, quiets us with love, and sings for joy over us.

It may be very difficult to imagine God so full of joy over you. This image is especially difficult for people who have been abandoned physically or emotionally by parents. You may have been unwanted. You may have been criticized and rejected. You may have been abused at the hands of the people you needed most to comfort you.

But we are not unwanted by God. We will not be rejected or abused by God.

God delights in us. God longs to quiet our agitation and anxiety with love. God is so glad we are alive. God sings for joy! The Creator of the Universe takes delight in us and sings for joy!

Do you delight in me, God?
Are you glad I'm alive?
You amaze me!
Help me, Father God,
to experience your protection.
Help me, Mother God,
to experience your nurture.
Quiet my anxious heart.
Sing to me, God.
Sing your songs of joy to me
until I am quieted with your love.
Amen

GOD IS NOT TIRED OF ME

The Lord is the everlasting God, the Creator of the ends of the earth. He will not grow tired or weary, and his understanding no one can fathom.
Isaiah 40:28

There are times during our struggle to heal when our emotions become intense and stay intense for what seems like a very long time. We feel like we rant and rave and weep for hour after hour, day after day. And we worry that the people in our lives who love and support us will grow tired and weary. Will we wear them out? Will they grow tired of the journey?

In those times when we fear the limits of those who love us, we need to remind ourselves that the Everlasting God does not grow tired or weary. We can pour our heart out to God over and over again. We can rage and weep. God listens without hurry or exhaustion. God will not tire of us.

And God understands. Beyond what we can understand or fathom, God sees and knows and understands.

We need to keep talking to the people who support us, but with an appreciation for their limits and boundaries. We also need to talk to God. We can speak our heart freely and fully to our Creator every day, every hour. God will not tire of us.

It sounds silly when I say it, Lord.
But sometimes I worry that I will wear you out.
Or bore you.
But you are Everlasting God.
Creator of the ends of the earth.
You do not grow weary.
Your understanding cannot be fathomed.
You understand.
You do not tire of me.
Thank you.
Amen

GOD CARRIES ME

He tends his flock like a shepherd:
He gathers the lambs in his arms
and carries them close to his heart;
he gently leads those that have young.
Isaiah 40:11

The Almighty God, Creator of heaven and earth, is pictured many times in the Bible as a Shepherd God. This may not be shocking to modern readers—most of us don't know much about sheep herding beyond the few sentimental ideas we may have about rural life. But nothing was more ordinary in biblical times that sheep herding. It was a dirty job. It was a low prestige job. A shepherd lived with his sheep. Day and night he was with them, paying attention to their needs, providing protection, and guiding them.

For the little ones in the flock—the most vulnerable ones—there was often a need for individual care and attention. In times of special need or danger, the shepherd would seek them out, lift them into his arms and carry them close to his heart.

This is how God cares for us. God is a God of gentleness, of tender affection, of protection, and of nurture. Our God is a Shepherd God. When we feel afraid or vulnerable, God is aware of our need. We are gathered into God's arms. We are carried close to God's heart.

I am your lamb, Lord.
The wolves are not far off.
Pick me up
and hold me
in your arms.
Carry me
close to your heart.
Allow me to experience
the mystery of being held
by your loving arms.
Amen

I pray that out of his glorious riches he may strengthen you with power through his Spirit in your inner being, so that Christ may dwell in your hearts through faith.
Ephesians 3:16

Sometimes recovery is exhausting. Sometimes we feel like a raw nerve all the way down to the core of our being. You can't touch anything without causing pain. In times like this we see clearly that our healing must be from the inside out. Nothing superficial will be of any consequence. We need our "inner being," our "heart," to experience God's healing power.

It is clear from this text that God understands where our healing must take place. The Spirit seeks to strengthen us in our "inner being." Christ seeks to dwell in our hearts. God is not interested in appearances. God is not interested in performances. It is not God's plan for us to look good. God's work will be deeper and necessarily more painful than this. The transformation we need will take place at the core of our being where Christ dwells in love and blessing.

This may seem impossibly difficult to us. But it is not impossible for God. It is out of "his glorious riches" that God can come to live within us.

I have worked hard
to look good on the outside, Lord.
But, it has done no good.
It hasn't worked.
I am not what I appear to be.
I need to heal from the inside.
Only you can do that, Lord.
Come, Holy Spirit, to my inner being.
Come, Christ, dwell in my heart.
Heal and strengthen me
in the depths of my person.
Out of your riches,
make your home in me.
Amen

*Which of you, if his son asks for bread, will give him a
stone? Or if he asks for a fish, will give him a snake? If you,
then though you are evil, know how to give good gifts to your
children, how much more will your Father in heaven give
good gifts to those who ask him!*
Matthew 7:9-11

Our children ask regularly for bread, milk, cereal and every
other kind of food in the house. We delight in their appe-
tite and their growth and development. It is pleasurable for us
to provide the basic good things they need to be nourished and
sustained physically.

Jesus uses the simple joys of parenting to make a point about
God. Just as parents enjoy providing for their children, God is
eager to provide good things for us. God is a good parent. God
delights in our growth, development and nurture. But God is
not a codependent parent. God wants us to ask directly for the
things we need. The importance of asking comes from the fact
that it requires us to acknowledge our need. We have learned to
deny our needs. We have learned to act as if we can take care of
ourselves. As a result, we have a difficult time both asking God for
good things and trusting God to respond.

Most of us begin with the struggle to identify our needs and to
put them into words. After this we struggle to acknowledge that
these needs can't be met with our own resources. And finally, we
struggle to come to God and to trust God to be a giver of good
gifts.

Lord, I acknowledge to you today
that I have many needs.
I cannot take care of these needs on my own.
I turn to you for help.
Giver of Good Gifts, hear my prayer.
I am in need of what only you can give.
Help me to trust you today.
Help me to rest in the promise
that you desire to give good gifts.
Open my eyes to see
and my heart to receive
your good gifts to me.
Amen

GOD LEADS WITH HUMAN KINDNESS

I led them with cords of human kindness,
with ties of love; I lifted the yoke from their neck
and bent down to feed them.
Hosea 11:4

We have all experienced a variety of leadership styles. Unfortunately we are most familiar with either the chaotic leadership of leaders-who-don't-lead or the rigid leadership of leaders-who-control-inappropriately.

Because we are so familiar with these dysfunctional leadership styles, we may not always expect God's leadership to be helpful. Sometimes we worry that God cannot be trusted to lead effectively in times of crisis or uncertainty. But God does not appear to have uncertainties about the role of Leader. God will lead us. God is familiar with this territory. God has charted these waters. God knows how to find water holes in this desert. God can find trails in this trackless wasteland. God can be trusted to lead.

God will lead us, but God will not lead with heavy-handed-ness and control. God does not lead using threats and punishments. God leads us with kindness and with love.

God is pictured in this text as a nurturing, attentive, kind parent. God lifts the burden off our back. God bends down and feeds us. We can trust God to lift from us the "yokes" that bind us. God will feed us. God will lead us with love.

Burden-lifter,
give me strength today.
God-of-Nurture,
give me nourishment today.
Lead me with kindness.
Tie me to you with love.
Amen

It is common for parents to tell about the time when their small child looked up into their face and asked "Are you God?" Little children form images of what the world is like, what they themselves are like, and what God is like through the interactions they have with their parents. Images are powerful mental pictures that are deeply rooted in us. If parents are consistent, compassionate, attentive and responsive to a child, the child will probably picture God as consistent, compassionate, attentive and responsive. If parents are neglectful, inconsistent or abusive, the child's perception of God will almost certainly include those traits.

Many people recognize early in the recovery process that they have acquired distorted images of God and that these images have a profound effect on their current relationship with God. But recognition does not by itself make the distortions disappear. It is a long and difficult struggle to replace images of a harsh and punitive God with images of God as trustworthy and loving.

But it is possible. God has, fortunately, revealed his character to us in clear terms. God is not a distant, unknowable God. God has come near to us, has been among us, has learned personally what it feels like to live on a fallen planet.

May God grant you insight to see clearly the ways in which your images of God have been distorted. May God grant you the courage to face the realities which have caused these distortions. And may you experience hope and joy as you learn to see God in new ways.

MAKING GOD IN MY IMAGE

Although they claimed to be wise, they became fools
and exchanged the glory of the immortal God
for images made to look like mortal man
and birds and animals and reptiles.
Romans 1:23

We do not take wood or stones and make idols. We do not pray to statues or prepare food for idols to eat.

It is not with our hands but with our imaginations that we carve out little gods to worship. Just like those who carve out idols with their hands, we make little gods out of our fear and ignorance. Our fundamental problem is that we imagine a God that comes out of our human experience. We imagine God to be like the people we have known in our lives. If we have been raised with impossible expectations, we may find ourselves worshipping the god-of-impossible-expectations. If we have experienced neglect, we may find ourselves in the service of the god-who-does-not-care. Since these gods do not respond to us when we call, we work harder and harder to please them. We try to be good. We try to be religious. But, we can never do enough. In this way we trade the "glory of the immortal God" for the very dysfunctional images which arise from our experiences with "mortal men."

The good news is that God is not the way we expect. The one true God, the immortal God, is a glorious God. God is a compassionate God, slow to anger, abounding in love and mercy.

Lord, you can see how I cling to my little gods.
I have tried so hard to please them.
But, they are harsh and abusive.
I cannot please them.
But I can't seem to get rid of them either.
They are awful little gods,
but they are all I know.
I have grown accustomed to them.
I have adapted my expectations
to match their smallness.
I am weary to death of the gods
who come from shame, Lord.
I long to worship you, God of Grace.
I long to worship you.
You are the God of Glory.
Give me eyes to see you more clearly today.
Give me a heart that hopes in you.

Amen

TURNING TO GOD FROM IDOLS

you turned to God from idols
to serve the living and true God
1 Thessalonians 1:9

It is remarkably easy for us to grow accustomed to false gods. We can develop a bizarre security in trying to please a god-who-will-not-be-pleased. We persist in the belief that if we keep trying, and keep working and keep attempting to control ourselves, we may finally be acceptable to our idol-god. But the trying and working and attempting to control never seem to work. Instead, we find ourselves re-enacting old family dramas. We find ourselves ever more deeply entrenched in shame, blame, rejection and self-loathing.

A remarkable thing can happen when we turn from our idols—from our false little gods—to serve the living and true God. It doesn't happen all at once. But gradually we unclench our tight fists. We open our closed hearts. We take in light. We take in love. It is like coming outside after being in a small, dark room. We walk outside and feel overwhelmed by the richness of the sky and land around us. We thought God was small and dreary. And we discover instead vastness and warmth.

The call to turn from our idols to the living and true God is a daily call. The old idol-gods will draw us back. We need to leave them over and over again. We need to turn again and again to the God who seeks to liberate us from their bondage.

I turn to you again today, God.
You are the Living and True God.
I leave my idol-gods again today.
I renounce the god-of-impossible expectations.
He is not God.
I renounce the god-who-is-eager-to-punish.
He is not God.
I renounce the god-who-keeps-his-distance.
He is not God.
I turn myself again today to you,
Living and True God.
I turn myself to you.
Amen

I keep asking that the God of our Lord Jesus Christ, the glorious Father, may give you the Spirit of wisdom and revelation, so that you may know him better.
Ephesians 1:17

P aul kept asking God that his friends would be able to know God better. He clearly did not think of the Christian life as a one-time event. This text assumes that to become a Christian is to enter a life-long process of learning to see and know God better.

The two things needed for this process are wisdom and revelation. Wisdom is something internal. During recovery the Spirit works within us to make us wise. This involves weeding out all of the distorted ideas and distorted thinking processes which supported our denial system. The Spirit is capable of removing our "stinking thinking" and making us wise.

The second thing we need in the recovery process is revelation. Revelation is external to us—it is God's self-disclosure to us. Without an external frame of reference, we are perfectly capable of creating a reality of our own choosing. Our denial is capable of creating a comprehensive alternate reality with no external checks or balances. The Spirit, however, works to reveal to us what is true, what is real. As a result we gradually learn that there is a reality beyond our pretense and denial.

The purpose of the Spirit's work is to help us grow in our capacity to know God.

I need wisdom. Lord.
Help me to be wise.
I need revelation, Lord.
Show me.
Let me see.
Spirit of Wisdom,
Spirit of Revelation,
fill my heart today
so that I may
know you better.
Amen

This will be a sign to you: You will find a baby wrapped in cloths and lying in a manger. . .and all who heard it were amazed at what the shepherds said to them.
Luke 2:12, 18

Some people think of God as a monster. Others think of God as the bully-in-the-sky. Others think of God as remote and abstract. These images come readily to us. We would not find it difficult to invent these gods. We are not amazed by them.

Like those who heard the shepherd's report, however, we stand amazed at the Christian Image. The image of a vulnerable God, a God-in-human-flesh, does not come readily to us. Who would have ever invented this God who comes as an infant? Who would have ever dared to think such a thing of God? But this is The Story, The Image. Christians have always insisted that the central drama of the history of this planet is centered on this God-who-comes-as-an-infant.

Things have not changed since the shepherds shared the amazing news. Being a Christian still involves staying open to the possibility that God will surprise us today. Just as God surprised the shepherds that day, so God may surprise us today.

Staying open to the possibility that God will surprise us with good things is not easy for people like us who find it easier to expect bad things. But God surprises us again and again with good things. The same God who came as a baby, wrapped up, lying in a feeding trough continues to surprise us.

What a surprise you are, God!
I expected monster,
bully,
distant abstraction.
What a surprise you are, Infant-God!
Help me this day to be open
to your surprising grace.
Help me this day to be open
to your surprising love.
Help me this day
to hope in you.
Help me to allow my deep longings
for you to awaken
so that I will not miss your surprises.
Amen

LIVING WITH PARTIAL VISION

*Now we see but a poor reflection as in a mirror; then we
shall see face to face. Now I know in part; then I shall know
fully, even as I am fully known.*
1 Corinthians 13:12

As we open ourselves to see and know God in new ways, we
will need to guard against using our relationship with God
as a new arena for expressing our perfectionism. We cannot now
see God except in a "poor reflection." We cannot perfectly know
God. We are not yet face to face with God. We see partially. We
know partially. There is much that remains a mystery to us.

It is not easy for us to live with partial vision. It is difficult to
tolerate the ambiguities and unknowns. Sometimes the imperfec-
tions in our understanding of God make us anxious. We feel that
God expects more of us than that. We feel that we should have
answers to every conceivable question, that we should never experience doubts, that we should have clarity at all times.

But this text makes it clear that 20:20 vision is not a realistic
expectation in our relationship with God. Perfection is not an
option for us. Accepting limits in our capacity to see and know
God is part of getting to know God better.

The list of things I don't understand
goes on and on, Lord.
What I don't know makes me anxious.
I am afraid of my doubts.
I want to see and know you so well
that I no longer experience doubt.
I want to understand things so thoroughly,
that I no longer experience anxiety.
But I cannot see you face to face.
I only see and know in part.
Help me, Lord,
to find a way to live
with uncertainty,
with doubts,
with anxiety.
Help me to embrace what you have revealed
of your love and goodness
and to live in anticipation of one day
knowing you fully.
Amen

*Dear friends, now we are children of God, and what we will
be has not yet been made known. But we know that when
he appears, we shall be like him, for we shall see him as he is.
Everyone who has this hope in him purifies himself, just as
he is pure.*
1 John 3:2-3

C hristians do not believe about life that "what you see is what
you get." Quite to the contrary, Christians believe that many
things we cannot now see are still part of God's plans for us. Some
days we cannot see—or maybe even imagine—what it would be
like to be completely recovered. But we know that this is God's
plan for us. God is committed to our full recovery. As this text
puts it, God will not be done with us until we are "like him." That
is as recovered as you can get.

The clarity of God's plan for us can give us hope. It may be a
difficult journey, but you can get somewhere from here. We can
make it because God is involved in the process of our transformation. This hope can give us a kind of purity of purpose and vision.
Because God is committed to our full recovery, we are not alone
with our hopes and dreams. Because God is committed to our full
recovery, we have a power greater than our own to help with the
struggle. Because God is committed to our full recovery, we can
find rest and courage in the purity of God's vision for us.

Because God is committed to our full recovery, we can let go
of our pathetic little idol gods and turn to the true and living
God. When we worshipped a god-of-impossible-expectations, we
became driven and compulsive. When we worshipped a god-who-
abused, we became fearful and frozen. When we worshipped a

god-who-keeps-his-distance, we fought despair. As we begin to see God as loving, we come to believe that we are lovable. As we begin to see that God wants us to let go of our self-destructive behaviors in order to live more fully, we come to believe that we are precious and valuable.

What I see, Lord,
is not always a very pretty picture.
I long for you to appear.
If you enter the picture, everything changes.
Seeing you changes everything
because when I see you,
I am changed.
Seeing you transforms me.
Sink this hope deep within me, Lord.
Purify me with this hope.
Thank you.
Amen

REST

Most of us are not very good at resting. If we even pause in life, we tend to get anxious. But if we slow down long enough to actually rest, emotional pain and trauma may start floating to the surface. To avoid this, we drive ourselves mercilessly. We keep the pace of life set at frenzy and hope that we have the energy to continue living this way for a long time.

We also avoid rest because we derive such a disproportionate sense of value in life from the things we do. We do and do and do in order to feel okay about ourselves. If we pause long enough to "be," we get agitated. If we slow down long enough to actually rest, we can become profoundly disoriented as we experience threats to our identity as a doer.

But we need rest. Rest restores us. It restores our bodies from the fatigue of constant activity and adrenaline rushes. It restores our minds from the never-ending clutter of lists of things to do. It restores our souls from the insanity of grandiose self-perceptions of being both indispensable and capable of performing beyond normal human limits.

God knows us better than we know ourselves. God knows we need rest. God considers rest to be so important that he tells us to rest. Rest honors God and restores our perspective. In resting we remind ourselves who is God and who is not.

May God give you the courage to rest. May you find ways to rest that will restore your soul.

REST AS DWELLING WITH GOD

He who dwells in the shelter of the Most High
will rest in the shadow of the Almighty
I will say of the Lord, "He is my refuge and my fortress,
my God, in whom I trust."
Psalm 91:1-2

I magine yourself traveling across a desert in the heat of the afternoon sun. You are desperate for a place to rest. You need shelter from the heat. You search the horizon for a tree or a large rock that could provide the comfort of shade.

During the process of recovery we become aware of our need for a sheltered place in which to rest. The journey can be exhausting and disorienting. But we don't know how to rest. It doesn't come naturally to us. We don't know where to find a safe shelter.

Now imagine yourself resting in God's shadow. You are sheltered, safe, at rest. The heat of the desert will not consume you because of God's protection. You can sit and rest in God's loving presence. God is a shade, a shelter, a fortress. You can draw strength and comfort from God's presence.

Rest has the potential of teaching us two essential truths. First, we are not God. God is God. We are creatures. We are limited, finite, dependent. It is a good thing to be a creature with needs. Second, when we rest we may learn in new ways that we are loved. Because we are God's children, God loves us. Not because of what we do, but simply because of who we are, we are loved.

I turn to you, Lord
from the heat of the sun
and the pressures of the journey of life.
I turn to you
for shelter
and refuge.
I want to rest in you today.
Be my shelter,
O Most High.
Amen

Come to me, all you who are weary and burdened, and I will give you rest. Take my yoke upon you and learn from me, for I am gentle and humble in heart, and you will find rest for your souls. For my yoke is easy and my burden is light.
Matthew 11:28-30

God desires to give us rest. But we resist this gift. No matter how badly we may want to rest, it is not an easy gift to receive. We may be weary. We may be burdened. But we are good at minimizing and avoiding our needs. As soon as we get this next task done, then we will rest. As soon as there is time for it, then we will rest. We want to rest, but we have to work real hard to make time for resting and then when we're back at work we will need to work real hard to make up for the "lost" time.

While we resist the gift of rest, many of us welcome burdens. We find it easier to believe that burdens are the gift God really wants to give us. We will welcome a difficult mission from God, a task, a challenge. We welcome the opportunity to wear ourselves out in ministry.

But the heavy burdens, the weariness, are not God's plan for us. God's burden is light. God's plan for us is not exhaustion but soul rest. God wants us to be so rested that being-at-rest sinks down to the foundations of our person. God wants us to be rested down to our souls. In rest we find that many of the burdens of life do not belong to us. We find the freedom to give back to God those things over which we have no control.

Give me the courage
to come and receive from you, Lord.
Burdens weigh heavy on my soul.
Give me the courage
to come and receive from you, Lord.
My restless soul longs for you.
Give me the courage
to come and receive from you, Lord.
Replace these burdens with your rest.
Share with me your easy yoke
so that I can find
rest for my soul.
Amen

REST AND EFFORT

There remains, then, a Sabbath-rest for the people of God;
for anyone who enters God's rest also rests from his own
work, just as God did from his. Let us, therefore, make every
effort to enter that rest . . . let us then approach the throne of
grace with confidence, so that we may receive mercy and find
grace to help us in our time of need.
Hebrews 4:9-11,16

God rested from his work. And God invites us to rest from ours. In our time of need God invites us to experience the rest-full-ness that comes from receiving mercy and grace.

But we resist. Rest is such a reversal of our expectations. We don't expect mercy and grace—we expect criticism. We don't expect to be invited to approach with confidence—we expect rejection. We don't expect rest—we expect to receive a list of demanding tasks to perform. Becoming the kind of people who are capable of rest will require us to change. It will require effort on our part.

First, we will need to change the way we see ourselves. We are attached to the illusion that we have no limits. We may not claim to be immortal, but if we examine our behavior, we act as if we need less rest than God. God rested. We don't. Clearly something is wrong. If we are to become the kind of people who are capable of rest, it will take some effort to change the way we see ourselves.

Second, to increase our capacity for rest, we will need to change our behavior. Rest is not an idea. It is a behavior. It will take some effort to change the way we live. We will need to learn the skills that make it possible for us to say "no" to over commitment. We will need to build rest into the rhythm of our lives. God rested. We need to do the same.

Help me to acknowledge my need for rest, Lord.
Help me to make quiet spaces in my life
when I cease all my doing
and allow myself to be.
Help me to make the effort to rest today.
Amen

REST WITHOUT COMPULSION

The Sabbath was made for man,
not man for the Sabbath.
Mark 2:27

The Sabbath is a day of rest. It is a day to stop working, to reflect, to remember, to celebrate. It is a day for quietness and a day for worship. God's concerns about the Sabbath do not come from a desire to control us. Jesus made it clear that Sabbath-keeping was not meant to be one more compulsion, one more "should," one more obligation. God does not ask us to rest because he wants to create one more burden for us.

Rest for people is like oil changes for internal combustion engines. A lot of careful engineering goes into the manufacturer's recommendations about oil changes. Maybe we can put it off for a while, but we can't put it off forever. The engine will stop working. Irreversible damage will be done. The manufacturer does not recommend oil changes because it has a vested interest in selling lots of oil. The manufacturer knows what the engine needs and wants it to run for us without breaking down.

God wants our experience with life to be a positive one. And God knows what we need for this to happen. God knows we can put off rest for a while, but we can not put it off forever. We will stop functioning. We will do irreversible damage.

Many of us have a history of taking days of rest and making them the most rest-less days of the week. We have an amazing ability to fill a day of rest with non-stop activity. But expressing our compulsivity in leisure activities is not the same thing as rest. It will take some creativity and discipline for us to find ways to keep the Sabbath that work for us. But that's what God wants.

God wants Sabbath to be "for" us. The Sabbath is God's gracious provision for us.

Help me not to become
compulsive about rest, Lord.
I am compulsive about
so many other things.
Spare me from adding this
to my long list of things to do.
You offer me rest, Lord,
because you love me.
Out of a growing love for you
and for myself
help me to allow myself
to rest today.
Amen

REST AND STRENGTH

In repentance and rest is your salvation,
in quietness and trust is your strength.
Isaiah 30:15

Our work is an important part of our identity. We have a legitimate need to contribute and to feel competent. Too often, however, this legitimate need is distorted by a compulsion to work. We work and work and work because we want to prove ourselves, because we want to feel capable and strong. When our identity and value are primarily wrapped up in our productivity it provides us with an appearance of strength. But this strength does not go deep—it is only a matter of appearances. The more we achieve or produce, the more anxious we become. We wonder when it will all come crashing down. We wonder when we will be found out.

This text suggests that strength comes from other sources. Probably the most surprising suggestions are that strength comes from quietness and that salvation comes from rest. Why would rest and quietness be so important?

Salvation is not possible when we are in charge because we are not the Messiah. We cannot save the world. We cannot even save ourselves. When we rest, we are forced to abandon our messianic illusions. When we rest we accept our place as creatures in need of being saved by someone with power greater than our own. When we do this, repentance comes and salvation is possible.

Quietness has a similar effect. We cannot hear what God has to say when our lives are full of noise. The frenzy of life can drown out God's voice. But when we rest, we can again hear God's voice. And it is God's words of love that can make us strong.

Lord, I am not very strong.
All my striving, and doing and proving
haven't made me strong.
I long for the deep strength
that comes from quietness
and from trust.
I rest my weary soul in you today, Lord.
Give me the courage to be quiet.
Give me the faith to trust in you.
Strengthen me today in your love.
Amen

REST AND JOY

All who keep the Sabbath without desecrating it
and who hold fast to my covenant -
these I will bring to my holy mountain
and give them joy in my house of prayer.
Isaiah 56:6b-7a

Rest can lead to joy because it creates a new perspective in us. Rest reminds us that we don't have to be compulsively responsible for the world and everything in it. Rest reminds us that God is in charge.

Rest also leads to joy because it leads to a renewed relationship with God. As this text puts it, God promises to lead Sabbath-keepers to his holy mountain. In rest we can be led to a place of joy in God's house of prayer. It is a beautiful image of God rejoicing with people who rest.

Rest can also lead to joy because it restores us. It renews and re-energizes us because it allows us to balance our "being" with our "doing." When we cease doing for a time, our senses are opened again to the world around us. We can see life with new gratitude and awe. And gratitude and awe produce joy.

Rest frees us to be what we are—creatures. We are creatures who can work and play, give and receive, weep and laugh. Today we can balance our working, giving and weeping with playing, receiving and laughing.

Lord, I want to stop
doing for a time today.
I want to stop
and remember that
you are God.
Help me to experience
the freedom and joy of being your creature.
Help to keep the Sabbath.
Bring me
to your holy mountain.
Give me joy
in your house of prayer.
Amen

HOPE

Hope is an essential ingredient of recovery. The day-to-day struggles of recovery are just too overwhelming for us if we do not have a source of hope. Without hope, we will find ourselves either distracted or in despair. With hope, we can find the courage and strength to continue. Hope makes it possible for us to do the work of healing because hope allows us to see our current struggles as an investment in the future.

There is a big difference, of course, between hope and "wishful thinking." Wishful thinking is rooted in denial—it is a pretending about the future. It cuts us off from our feelings by offering a reality in which we feel only pleasant emotions and everyone lives happily ever after. Wishful thinking is easy. But it has no real substance. It will not satisfy us.

The experience of hope begins to take root in us when we start to break out of the denial that has ruled our lives. Ironically, therefore, it is just when things seem impossible and we feel completely helpless that real hope first becomes possible. Facing the reality of our present circumstances and facing the fact that we do not control the future—this is the difficult soil in which hope grows. But hope can grow. The God of Hope is eager to give us the gift of hope. God has plans for us. They may not have the fairy-tale endings we wish for, but God has good plans for us. The hope we need can come from knowing that God is greater than our disappointments, greater than our failures, greater than our brokenness.

May the God of Hope give you the courage to hope again today.

Then they led him away to crucify him.
Matthew 27:31

There are days when it is difficult, if not impossible, to sustain hope. The day of Jesus' death was such a day. It was a day of despair for all who had put their hope in him. It was a day of unbearable grief for those who had been changed by his love. In such terrible moments hope disappears. Darkness seems to be all that remains. God seems absent.

It is, however, one of the most fundamental convictions of the Christian faith that—in those times when hope seems unattainable—God is at work. In that moment when even Jesus had a difficult time sustaining hope in God's redemptive purposes, God was fighting the decisive battle which would make it possible for God's love to reach to all. In that moment of terror, the foundations of reality were exposed and God was at work on the deep structures of the world. God could do work at that moment which would have been impossible during ordinary times.

Much the same is true of our moments of hopelessness. It is when hope grows weakest that our foundations are most exposed. It is when the struggle to sustain hope is most difficult that God can work on the deep structure of our persons. It is at those times that God can reach the unreachable crevices of our hearts and work on regions where fear and despair seem to reign.

It is a terrible thing to lose hope. But all is not lost. Though we lose hope, God is still at work. It may be that during our season of hopelessness God will extend the rule of the Kingdom of God into new regions of our lives.

In those times when I cannot hope, Lord,
help me to remember the work which
you accomplished during Jesus' hour of darkness.
Remind me, when I lose all hope,
that all hope is not gone
because you continue your work in me.
Extend your rule into the deepest regions of my heart
where fear and despair
have reigned for too long.
Amen

*because of the tender mercy of our God, by which the rising
sun will come to us from heaven to shine on those living in
darkness and in the shadow of death to guide our feet into
the path of peace*
Luke 1:78-79

Many of us grew up expecting bad things. Some of us learned to expect physical abuse. As a result we may find ourselves covering our heads to ward off a blow when someone is offering a hug. Others of us learned to expect to be neglected. As a result we may experience confusion or fear when someone shows an interest in getting to know us. Expectations which are formed early in life are difficult for us to change. It is not an easy thing to allow ourselves to hope when our hopes have been disappointed over and over again in the past.

Learning to hope, however, means opening ourselves to the possibility that the future may be different from what we have known in the past. To hope is to allow ourselves to anticipate the possibility of good things. Hope is the expectation of good. It is the ability to look for the rising of the sun, while sitting in the predawn darkness.

Our hope for the future is rooted in a conviction about God's character. It is because of God's tender mercies that we find it possible to hope. Because of God's character—tender and full of mercy—the sun will rise. We can anticipate good things because God is a good and loving God.

*I know what it is like
to live in darkness, Lord.
My house has been built
in the shadow of death.
God of mercy,
heal me.
God of tenderness,
give light.
Build in me a capacity for hope.
Rise on my darkness, Lord.
Guide my feet
out of
the paths of fear
and into
the path of peace.
Amen*

HOPE AND THE PAST

I will remember the deeds of the Lord;
yes, I will remember your miracles of long ago.
I will meditate on all your works
and consider all your mighty deeds.
Psalm 77:11-12

Sometimes hope fails us because of the pain of present circumstances. The intensity of the daily struggle can overwhelm us and crowd out hope for the future. We find ourselves unable to focus on a hope-full future because we cannot see beyond the burdens of the present. But we need hope in order to continue the journey. Without it we cannot go on. Without hope there is only the despair that comes when we think nothing will ever change.

Reviewing our experiences of God's help in the past is one way of nurturing hope. When present events crowd out hope, leaving despair and fear, we can turn to the disciplines of remembering. It can sustain our faith and renew our determination to continue the journey.

Remembering is not an easy discipline for us. Our memory is not good. Even miracles seem to age quickly—they become "miracles of long ago." Things that seemed unimaginably wonderful at the time can quickly fade in our memory as present concerns demand our attention. Dramatic breakthroughs in recovery that seemed to be powerful signs of God's grace and presence may seem painfully ordinary after a few months. For this reason it may be necessary to find someone to help us with the discipline of remembering. Hope can often be renewed by asking a trusted friend to remind us where we have been. An objective review of the journey to this point helps us see God's sustaining grace in our lives. And that gives us the hope to go on.

Lord, help me to remember
the specific ways
you have sustained
me in the past.
Help me to remember
how I have changed.
Help me to remember
your love and grace
so that I can grow
in my capacity for hope today.
Amen

HOPE AND THE PRESENT

Those who hope in the Lord
will renew their strength.
They will soar on wings like eagles;
they will run and not grow weary,
they will walk and not be faint.
Isaiah 40:31

Hope gives us strength. We need strength for the journey of recovery. We need strength to make the changes that need to be made—and strength to grieve the losses which come with change. We need strength to keep on keeping on. Recovery requires a great deal of physical, emotional and spiritual strength. We draw that strength day-to-day from hope.

There are times when hope will allow us to soar. We will feel the exhilaration of change and new freedom. We will think about the future and imagine good things. We will soar with gratitude and joy because of hope.

There are other times when hope will allow us to run and not grow weary. We will keep going. Keep changing. Keep working. Keep feeling. We may get tired but hope will keep us from getting weary and wanting to give up. Hope helps us to keep running.

There are other times when hope will allow us to walk without fainting. Some days, in our recovery journey, continuing the journey at all is very difficult. The struggle we face may be so intense that we would faint if it were not for hope. But hope helps us to take the next step.

Thank you, Lord,
for the gift of hope.
Thank you for
the days when hope
allows me to soar.
And for the days when it
allows me to keep running.
And thank you
for the days when hope
gives me the courage
to walk without fainting.
Thank you for hope.
Amen

HOPE AND THE FUTURE

"For I know the plans I have for you," declares the Lord,
"plans to prosper you and not to harm you, plans to give you
hope and a future."
Jeremiah 29:11

Hope is about the future. It may be oriented to the next hour, or the next day, or the next month or year or decade. But hope is always about anticipation.

Those of us who like to control things often find hope difficult because we do not control the future. Many of us are compulsive makers-of-plans. We are willing to work ourselves to death trying to make our plans become reality. But when our hopes and vision for the future are based only on what we can control, our vision is inevitably narrowed and impoverished.

We need to remind ourselves regularly, therefore, that God's vision for the future is better than our own. God sees possibilities and opportunities that we cannot see. The horizons of God's imagination are not bounded. When we root our hope in God, a totally different future is possible. It is not a future we can control. God's plans may not be the same as our plans. But we can return again and again to God as our source of hope.

God has been clear about our future. It is God's intention to give us a hope and a future. This is not a promise of a trouble-free life. It is not a promise of immunity from struggle. But it is a promise of hope. God has been with us in the past. God is with us in the present. And God will be with us in the future.

Thank you for paying attention
to my future, Lord.
Thank you for making plans.
Help me today to rest
in the thought that
your plans for me include blessing.
Open my heart today
to the hope
and the future
you have prepared for me.
Amen

May the God of hope fill you with all joy and peace as you
trust in him, so that you may overflow with hope by the
power of the Holy Spirit.
Romans 15:13

Hope does not come as the just reward for our hard work and struggle. It comes as a gift. The experience of hope is very much like the experience of receiving a surprise gift that is perfectly suited to our needs. A really good gift is one that fits perfectly both the giver and the receiver. Hope fits our needs perfectly. But if a gift is out-of-character with the giver, then it may be difficult for the receiver to accept without reservations. Fortunately, hope is just the kind of gift that fits God's character. It is a perfect fit for God. The God of Hope loves to give hope.

We need to remind ourselves daily that we do not serve the god-of-relentless-cheerfulness, or the god-of-naivete, or the god-of-blind-optimism. We serve the God of Hope. God is hope-full and loves to share hope-full-ness with us. We can come to God with our fear, doubt and despair and God will give good gifts to us. When all other reasons for hope fail us, we can return to the God of Hope because God is greater than our disappointment, greater than our failure, greater than the problems and conflicts in our hearts and our homes and our communities and our world.

Surprise me today, Lord.
Surprise me with hope.
Open my eyes
to see you clearly.
Help me
to see your hope-full-ness.
By the power of the Holy Spirit,
cause me to overflow
with hope.
Amen

Many of us have pretended to be happy for so long that we have forgotten what joy is all about. People ask "How are you?". We answer "Fine." With years of practice, our repertoire of emotions has narrowed to a small and tiresome little collection of things like "fine" and "okay." Sometimes when we actually feel anxious or guilty or angry, we think we need emotional anesthetics in order to control the intensity of our emotions. But the anesthetics for emotional pain are also powerfully effective against joy.

In the process of recovery we gradually find ourselves experiencing many new emotions. Early in recovery it may seem like all of these new emotions are painful ones. It is the pain which we have avoided for so long that we see most clearly at first. The pain necessarily comes first. Most of us will experience an increased capacity for sadness and anger long before we are surprised by our new capacity for joy. But recovery is about joy. Our capacity for joy and serenity and peace do increase during recovery. Joy does come. And, when it comes, it will be the real thing—not some pale, imitation, joy-like experience.

We cannot, of course, control joy. It does not come at our call. It does not stay at our command. More often than not, we are surprised by joy. Joy is fundamentally a gift from God. As we sink our roots more deeply in the soil of God's love, we find ourselves more able to receive from God. And as a result we find joy that we never thought possible.

May God increase your capacity for joy today. May God surprise you with joy.

The Son of Man came eating and drinking,
and you say, 'Here is a glutton and a drunkard,
a friend of tax collectors and "sinners."'
Luke 7:33-34

O ne of the accusations made by the religious leaders of Jesus' day was that he partied with undesirables. It was unacceptable in their minds to associate in any way with undesirables. That would make you unclean. But it was particularly unacceptable to party with undesirables. Then, as now, religion was thought to be very serious business, much too serious for the kind of celebrations that Jesus enjoyed. Religion was supposed to be about intellectual abstractions and theological detail—not about going to dinner parties with unsavory characters.

Jesus told many stories about God's love for celebration. When the lost is found, the finder throws a feast. When the prodigal returns, the father has a party. When a single person repents, the angels rejoice. And on and on. Jesus, the man of sorrows, was also a man of celebration and joy.

Like the religious leaders of Jesus' day, we may sometimes find ourselves resistant to joy. We may resist joy because we fear disappointment. Or we may resist joy because it doesn't seem congruent with being a serious-minded person of faith. We may resist joy because we have been shamed or even punished for being overly enthusiastic as a child.

It is a risk to make room for joy in our lives. Joy requires that we be open to the possibility of experiencing conflicting emotions. If we wait to experience joy until our anger, grief and self-condemnation are completely gone, then we will wait a long time. But it is possible to experience joy without denying or avoiding other more painful emotions. We can follow Jesus' example of joy today. When joy comes, we can receive it. It is a good gift from God.

Lord of joy,
Lord of celebration,
open my heart to the possibility of joy today.
Help me to tolerate the confusion
that comes when sorrow and joy
live side by side in my heart.
Give me the courage to
joyfully celebrate life.
Amen

FROM GRIEF TO JOY

You turned my wailing into dancing;
you removed my sackcloth and clothed me with joy,
that my heart may sing to you and not be silent.
Psalm 30:11,12

Sometimes it can seem that all there is to life is grief. We face painful realities and allow ourselves to feel the painful feelings. But grief is only for a season. There will come a season for joy. In fact one of the most surprising things about the recovery process is that as we grow in our capacity for experiencing deep emotional pain we also enlarge our capacity for experiencing joy. Recovery is not just about learning to experience unpleasant emotions. It is about learning to feel the full range of life's emotions.

Imagine for a moment that you are "clothed" in grief. God grieves with you. It is a time for wailing. Few words pass between you. But there is a great deal of emotion. Then, one day God brings you a new set of clothes. They are the clothes of joy. The time comes to change clothes. Your heart begins to sing. The time of wailing is over. The time for dancing has come.

Who can say how long this will take? It certainly cannot be rushed. But God is prepared to be with us through the whole process. God comforts us in grief. And God clothes us with joy and teaches us to dance and sing.

For teaching me to dance, Lord,
I give you thanks.
You are a good teacher.
My heart dances before you, Lord.
Your goodness endures forever.

For teaching me to sing, Lord,
I am grateful.
You are a good teacher.
My heart sings to you, Lord.
Your goodness endures forever.
Amen

JOY AND SHAME

*Jesus, the author and perfecter of our faith, who for the joy
set before him endured the cross, scorning its shame.*
Hebrews 12:2

S hame does not coexist comfortably with joy. Experiences of
shame eat away at the spiritual and emotional foundations on
which joy is built. When we are consumed by shame, joy will keep
its distance. But shame has a way of getting to us. Our defenses
against the clever tactics of shame are not well developed.

Jesus is a powerful example to us of how to resist shame and
make room for joy. First, Jesus "scorned" shame. He did not give
it a stature which it did not deserve. Experiences of shame did not
define who he was. He was not just the sum of the shame he had
experienced in life. His identity and person were securely rooted
in God. So, he was able to experience shaming experiences without internalizing the shame.

Secondly, Jesus had "joy set before him." Experiences of shame
hurt us. But we are not entirely defenseless. Jesus drew strength
to reject shame from the anticipation of joy. We can let go of our
shame when we allow ourselves to remember that God has plans
for us that include joy. We are not aimlessly adrift in life, headed
nowhere, wanderers in a meaningless maze. On the contrary,
every day takes us closer to the fulfillment of God's purposes.
Jesus' followers share his conviction that joy, not shame, is God's
purpose in creation. Today we can root ourselves in God's love for
us. We can scorn the shame. We can remind ourselves that God's
plans for us include joy.

Help me to scorn shame, Lord.
Help me to root myself
so completely in you
that shame has
no power over me.
Help me to see the joy you have set before me, Lord.
Remind me today of your plans.
Help me to draw strength today
from the hope that
your plans for me include joy.
Amen

JOY AND GRATITUDE

Praise the Lord, O my soul;
all my inmost being,
praise his holy name.
Psalm 103:1

There comes a time in the process of recovery when we find ourselves seeing life in an entirely different way. Along with the pain, we sense with increased clarity that life is fundamentally a good gift from God. This is the experience of gratitude. Gratitude is a kind of participation in and response to God's grace. Without it, recovery would be a cheerless, and probably impossible journey.

The experience of gratitude is a response of our inmost being to God's grace. When gratitude breaks through, we are able to stop our frantic efforts to earn our way through life. In these moments of calm we see that our inmost being belongs to God. We are God's creation. Sometimes that is all we need. Other times this thought that we are God's dearly loved creation is so far beyond all we could ever have asked, hoped or dreamed for, that our hearts fill with praise and joy.

Sometimes we try to force gratitude on ourselves. Sometimes other people try to force it on us. But it cannot be coerced. It will not come from pretending. It will not come from telling ourselves that some people are worse off than we are. But it does come. And, when it comes, it breaks through our pain and surprises us with joy.

We cannot force gratitude today. But we can allow ourselves to notice the many gifts God gives to us each day. We can open our hearts to receive these good gifts with simple expressions of thanks. As we do, our gratitude will be nurtured and our joy will grow.

Give me a capacity for gratitude today, Lord.
Break through the clouds of pain in my life.
Surprise me with joy.
Fill my soul, my inmost being,
with gratitude for life
and with praise to you.
Amen

Suppose a woman has ten silver coins and loses one. Does she not light a lamp, sweep the house and search carefully until she finds it? And when she finds it, she calls her friends and neighbors together and says, 'Rejoice with me; I have found my lost coin.' In the same way, I tell you, there is rejoicing in the presence of the angels of God over one sinner who repents.
Luke 15:8

There are lots of ways to be lost. Some of us are lost in the way a lost coin is lost. We have been knocked off the dresser and have rolled into a dark and dusty corner of the room. A lost treasure. A lost coin can't do much to get help. It's just lost. It can't call for help. It can't do anything to make things different.

Like the woman in this story, God notices that we are missing. God lights a lamp and searches for us. God keeps searching until we are found. The God who searches so carefully and persistently for the lost coin sees us as valuable, as a treasure. So, when we are found, God rejoices.

God is our Good Father. God values us. Even when we are unable to call for help—just like a lost coin—God searches for us. When we are found, it brings God great joy.

Lord, help me to take it in.
I can't imagine myself
as the object of your joy.
Help me to see
that you
find joy
in me.
Amen

JOY AND LOVE

Remain in my love. . . I have told you this so that my joy
may be in you and that your joy may be complete.
John 15:10-11

It is sometimes difficult to imagine joy at all. When we struggle with failure, or we are faced with our need for change or we are grieving old losses—in those times joy seems unimaginable.

But joy can come in the midst of these struggles as we learn what it means to remain in Jesus' love.

We do not have to grieve or change alone. We learn early in recovery that we will not get very far if we remain isolated. We also learn early that we need to turn to a power that is greater than ourselves. To recover we need to learn to remain—or abide or spend time—in the love Jesus gives us. We are loved by God. And we are loved by other people. It is in these loving relationships that we find joy.

In John 15 Jesus has been describing himself as the vine, telling us that we are branches. He is our life-line. We need to stay closely connected to him. We can no longer pretend to be self sufficient. We can daily acknowledge our need for God's healing love.

Jesus told us this truth because he wanted us to experience joy. "Remain in my love," Jesus said, "so your joy will be complete."

Lord, help me to remain in love.
Help me not to distance myself
from you or from others.
Help me to give up
pretending to be self sufficient.
Help me to remember that it is
in loving
and in being loved
that I will find
healing and joy.
Amen

Visit the virtual home of the
National Association for Christian Recovery!
Online discussion groups, an extensive library,
audiotapes of conference presentations, a daily
meditation by email (taken from *Rooted in God's
Love*) and lots of other good stuff.

Made in the USA
Charleston, SC
18 March 2012